DOES THE BIBLE REALLY SAY THAT? SERIES

YOUR TRUE SELF IDENTITY

DOES THE BIBLE REALLY SAY THAT? SERIES

YOUR TRUE SELF IDENTITY

How Familiar Translations
Of Bible Verses
In the Gospel of Matthew
Hide Your True Identity from You

Kalinda Rose Stevenson, Ph.D.

ABKA
ABKA Publishing

To Jim, with love

To Jane with love

Where all are guilty, no one is; confessions of collective guilt are the best possible safeguard against the discovery of culprits, and the very magnitude of the crime the best excuse for doing nothing.

Hannah Arendt

Contents

PART FOUR MIRRORS OF YOUR IDENTITY

PART FIVE THE IDENTITY OF JESUS IN MATTHEW

PART SIX IDENTITY QUESTIONS OF THE HERO

PART SEVEN IDENTITIES OF THOSE WHO TRAP LITTLE ONES

PART EIGHT FREEDOM TO BECOME YOUR TRUE SELF

Foreword

Who am I? At some point in all our lives we ask this question and we come up with many answers, father, mother, husband, wife, son, or daughter. But none of those answer the existential question of who we really are. For many, the Bible provides the answer and often our identity with a biblical definition starts at a very early age.

I have the experience of being born to a Muslim father and Christian mother. Who am I? Some of my first memories are learning the song "Jesus Loves Me."

> Jesus loves me this I know
>
> For the bible tells me so
>
> Little ones to Him belong
>
> I am weak but He is strong

And later in the song:

> Jesus loves me when I'm good
>
> When I do the things I should
>
> Jesus loves me when I'm bad
>
> Though it makes Him very sad

From the beginning, I learn that I am weak and must rely on someone else and that I make Jesus sad when I do things that others think are bad. I'm introduced to the idea of sin. But as I get older, I learn that I was born a sinner because of an idea of an original sin, committed by people in the Garden of Eden—a sin so complete that it continues to mark all humanity to this very day.

To accept Christianity is to accept that no matter who I become, my first identity will always be that of a sinner. If I question my identity or denounce it, I get another label: non-believer.

I've spent over thirty years now studying influence and persuasion and have written a number of books on the topic. One of the most powerful tools in a persuasive arsenal is a label. Labels are easy to read and understand, they are highly charged and very defining therefore easy to apply. Sinner. Saint. Holy Roller. All labels whispered in reverence or spit as an epitaph, but easy to identify in any case and accept or apply in judgment. Labels are particularly dangerous because they contain so much emotion and meaning derived from the story that is consolidated into the label. And they are accepted because they are polarizing. We want to be one of "those" but not "one of them."

Labels consolidate the essence, the emotion, the moral of the stories we are told. The most persuasive stories always follow a similar path, the *hero's journey*. Joseph Campbell best described the hero's journey and demonstrated how all religions followed the same path through their evolution. If the story is good enough, most people will believe and follow. The story can be condensed into an easy label like "saved" . . . no matter how the story started. The majority will never question the story.

Stories are designed for us to see ourselves in them. As they are told and retold, we see ourselves more like the hero on the journey and rarely as the adversary. It is much easier for a "hero" to apply a label to an adversary that everyone can agree to than vice versa. The best stories are loved and retold because they seem to hold a moral we should all agree on. Yet rarely are they dissected, torn apart, questioned. But when biblical stories are dissected and questioned, they become something else.

You'll be surprised when you read what Kalinda has to say about Matthew 18:6. What you learn there will set the stage for your own transformation. This is the part of the hero's journey where you experience death metaphorically.

But don't worry. Resurrection and rebirth follow quickly. You'll discover that those are very real!

Throughout this book, Kalinda challenges you to deconstruct the stories you've walked through again and again and find the authentic you. Not the "you" that reflects the essence and emotions of someone else's story that has been idealized to fit "every one." She challenges you to reject the role projected on you and accept the challenge that being *you* offers. As you read, you'll find yourself alternatively amazed by the mistranslated Bible verses that have led you to the place you are today and then nearly overwhelmed by who you might be, can be . . . even who you are.

This gives you the space to find the answer to the question of "Who are you?" And that answer is the basis for a life worth living.

I wish you great success and adventure as you uncover the *you* that has been covered up by mistranslated and misunderstood Bible verses and years of compelling but incomplete Bible stories. I hope the story you create is one that offers you something you can be(lieve) compelled by for the rest of your life.

Dave Lakhani

Author of *Persuasion: The Art of Getting What You Want and*

Subliminal Persuasion: Influence And Marketing Secrets They Don't Want You To Know

Preface
Bible Translations
and
Your Identity

How do you penetrate years, centuries,
of historical distortion to find original
truth?
Robert Langdon, *The DaVinci Code* film

Why Bible Translations Matter to Your Identity

Does The Bible Really Say That? Series focuses on the
influence of Bible translations on what you believe "the
Bible says" on any topic.

This series makes no claims about whether or not any
part of the Bible is historically true or false. The focus is
not on the Bible itself but the impact of claims about "what
the Bible says" on human readers of the Bible.

Bible believers study the Bible as the authoritative
guide to their lives. Non-believers quote the Bible to
ridicule its claims or denounce its relevance to
contemporary life. Both believers and non-believers alike
use the language of "the Bible says" to make their claims.

Does the Bible Really Say That? Series books focus on
the blind spot in such language. Unless readers are able to
read the Bible in its original languages, all of these claims
about "what the Bible says" are based on translations of
ancient documents. The result is that original meanings get
lost in translation. What "the Bible says" in its original
languages is not always what translations claim that "the
Bible says" on any particular topic. The result is often that

xvii

Bible readers experience self-conflict, confusion, and shame caused by misuse of the Bible.

Your True Self Identity: How Familiar Translations of Bible Verses in the Gospel of Matthew Hide Your True Identity from You focuses on the influence of Bible translations to shape what you believe the Bible says about your identity.

Why focus on translations of the Bible?

The first reason is that my own expertise comes from my training as a biblical scholar to look very carefully at the Bible in its original languages. I realize that most people don't share my fascination with the minute details of grammar and syntax and the meanings of words. I also know that the clues to historical distortions of Bible verses often lie obscured in the tiniest grammatical and linguistic details.

I am also aware that few Christian Bible readers understand the complexities of Bible translations and the power of Bible translators to determine what appears on the pages of their translated Bibles.

The simple truth is that THE Bible does not exist. Instead, Bibles exist in multiple translations, in multiple languages, based on multiple manuscript traditions. As a result, no two translations are alike.

If this is not enough complication, the Bible itself is made up a collection of separate books. Although we refer to the book by a singular name, *the Bible*, the word itself means "books." The Bible is a collection of smaller books, not a unified whole. In turn, many of the books contained in the Bible are composites of other writings.

The result is that the Bible resembles a tapestry. Tapestries are made from multiple strands woven together to create elaborate designs. In more contemporary terms— for those of us who don't have tapestries hanging on the walls of our homes—the Bible is something like a graphic created by Photoshop. Photoshopped images are often made up of multiple layers. The final graphic is usually one single image, but the image itself was created out of many layers. Layers can be separated out, changed, and then added back into the final image.

All of this means that translators start with complex and composite collections of ancient writings—various Bible manuscripts in ancient languages—and then translate them into a wide variety of new Bible tapestries called translations.

Translating any part of the Bible is extraordinarily difficult. How does anyone know with certainty the intended meanings and nuances of words in ancient languages? How does anyone convey original meanings of words and concepts into contemporary languages? Because careful translation involves enormous amounts of diligent work, most contemporary translations are the work of committees. As a result, the resulting translations are not always consistent within themselves concerning translation choices.

The Role of Translators

My focus is on the role of translators to choose the words you read on the pages of your Bible and how these translation choices define who you think you are.

Since Bible translators control the flow of data between ancient Bible manuscripts and the words you read on the pages of your translated Bibles, Bible translators have the capacity to distort original meanings of Bible verses concerning your identity. Even with the best intentions, translators are affected by unconscious assumptions, unquestioned beliefs, cultural blind spots, theological intentions, and particular purposes.

In other words, translators are finite and fallible human beings who are attempting to convey ancient words from ancient manuscripts into meaningful words for contemporary readers for their own particular historical and theological reasons.

My goal in this book is to identify places where the translators have misled readers by their translation choices. My particular focus is on specific misleading translation choices in Chapter 18 of the Gospel of Matthew. Whether or not these misleading translation choices are intentional or unintentional, Bible translation choices can hide your true self identity from you by mistranslating familiar Bible verses.

Overcoming Religious Education

Beyond the expertise I gained from my own professional training as a biblical scholar, my deepest motivation for this work comes from my lived experience of being an abused child. Beyond the abuse I endured within my own family, my experience was that the Christian church made my life situation worse.

In his book, *Further along the Road Less Traveled,* Scott Peck makes this statement:

> I sometimes tell people that one of the great blessings of my life was an almost total absence of religious education, because I had nothing to overcome (Peck 112).

Although it is impossible to know what might have been, my childhood experience of religious education only reinforced the abuse heaped upon me. In my case, my religious education gave me a whole lot to overcome. In my late teen and early adult years, as I began to seek help within the Christian church, the counsel I got from clergy and well-meaning lay people was no help at all.

If I were the only child who grew up terrified at home and terrified at church, I would have no reason to challenge what "everyone knows to be true" about the Bible. But I have met too many people who have been robbed of their true self identities by mistranslated Bible verses to remain silent.

My particular focus in this book is on the effect of translation choices on the most vulnerable. The vulnerable includes any of us who started life as children—which means all of us.

My purpose is to remove the guilty label from the innocent and to provide a better mirror for those whose true self identities have been hidden from them by misleading Bible translations.

Acknowledgments

This book would not exist without the endless patience, enthusiasm, and unwavering support of my husband Jim. He continues to be my devoted and steadfast companion on our long life journey together. He is the one who heard every idea in this book long before it took shape in the finished book.

He is also my resident technogeek, whose ability to decipher the mysteries of computer and software systems has enabled me to become an *almost* proficient technogeek.

I also want to acknowledge Dean Kloter, a customer who bought one of my earlier books and sent me an email before he had finished reading the whole book to tell me that the book had already changed his life. What higher affirmation can any author have than to know that the sometimes lonely and frustrating process of writing and publishing a book can have such an effect on a reader?

At the time, I was about ready to abandon my efforts to finish this book. Finding a way to challenge what "everyone knows is true" about the Bible, in a way that is both rigorous in scholarship and compassionate in tone, has often felt like an impossible task. Dean gave me a reason to finish.

I also thank Dean for reading an earlier version of the manuscript and his enthusiastic support to publish this book.

In addition, I thank Peggy Stevens, my longtime friend, for her insightful comments about an early version of the book. After many years of drinking tea together over long conversations about movies, religion and science, and the deer, wild turkeys, and occasional coyote that appeared on her hillside, I knew that I could trust her judgment.

Last, but by no means least, Dave Lakhani has been both mentor and friend to me. The mentor on a hero's journey provides essential gifts for the journey. Of all of Dave's gifts to me, both directly through conversations and emails, and indirectly through his books, the greatest gift that encompasses all of the rest is Dave's own heroic determination to be bold and to tell the truth, and his encouragement for me to do the same.

Prologue
A Story of Mistaken Identity

I never dreamed of such happiness as
this, while I was an ugly duckling.
"The Ugly Duckling"
Hans Christian Andersen

The Swan Who Thinks He's a Duck

"The Ugly Duckling" is one of Hans Christian Andersen's well-known stories. It's about a swan who doesn't know that he is a swan. He thinks he is a duck because he is hatched with ducks, and everyone calls him a duck. His life story is a miserable experience of being treated cruelly because he is unlike the other ducklings. He is the "ugly duckling." In all of this, he doesn't know his true identity. He thinks that he is a defective duck.

His young life as an ugly duckling in the barnyard is full of misery until the day he decides to escape:

> So it went on from day to day till it got worse and worse. The poor duckling was driven about by every one; even his brothers and sisters were unkind to him, and would say, 'Ah, you ugly creature, I wish the cat would get you,' and his mother said she wished he had never been born. The ducks pecked him, the chickens beat him, and the girl who fed the poultry kicked him with her feet. So at last he ran away, frightening the little birds in the hedges as he flew over the palings (Andersen, "The Ugly Duckling").

This well-loved story endures because it touches a deep wound in many of us—maybe all of us in one way or another. Most of us know what it feels like to be an ugly duckling. Throughout human history, people have been

1

judged defective because they are somehow *different* and that difference is judged as evidence of defectiveness.

[You can read the whole story of "The Ugly Duckling" by using the link provided in References.]

The Secret of Happiness

The ugly duckling's misery ends when he sees himself as he truly is for the first time in his life. He discovers his true self. He is not a duck. He is a swan. He was always a swan but he never knew it. At that moment, his life is transformed forever. Transformation is not a matter of turning into something you are not. Transformation occurs when you become your true self.

At the moment he knows his true identity for the first time, he is happy for the first time in his life. This little story conveys the real secret of happiness. Happiness is as close as being what you already are and as far away as trying to be something you are not. Unhappiness is trying to be a duck when you are really a swan. Or trying to be a swan when you are really a duck.

Here's my premise. You are already perfect. There is nothing at all wrong with you except that you don't know your true self identity. You don't need to change into something else. You need only become what you truly are. Sounds simple enough, doesn't it? But why is it so hard to do?

The Salvation Trap

Your True Self Identity identifies one reason. It's not the only reason, but this reason is so powerful, so pervasive, so influential, and so unchallenged that it has affected almost all of us in one way or another. It's the Christian doctrine of *original sin* and the salvation theology shaped by this doctrine of original sin. Together, this nefarious pair of doctrines turns every human being into an ugly duckling and then throws away the mirror. I call the result *the salvation trap.*

The salvation trap does what all traps do. It keeps you stuck in a place of no escape—until you find a way to get out of the trap. My purpose is to show you how to get out of the trap and set yourself free. It's easy when you realize the flimsiness of the trap.

Traps come in all forms. Some traps are things you can see and touch. Other traps are invisible constructions of beliefs and feelings. Each type of trap can keep you stuck. However, only the trap made up of beliefs and feelings can keep you stuck even if you run away.

When Flying Away Is Not Enough

Andersen's ugly duckling is trapped by his belief that he is an ugly duck. He is so tormented in the barnyard that he flies away, but he can't get out of the trap created by his belief that he is an ugly duck.

His escape from the barnyard is the beginning of his journey. Life doesn't get much better for him, as he meets wild ducks and geese—they all tell him how ugly he is. He has a terrifying encounter with a hunting dog. He endures a violent storm. Then he finds a ramshackle cottage inhabited by an old woman, a tomcat, and a hen. But he finds no home in that place, because he cannot purr the way the tomcat does or lay eggs the way the hen does.

The hen gives him this warning, expressed with the certitude of someone who knows what is best for the ugly duckling's own good:.

> We don't understand you? Who can understand you,
> I wonder? Do you consider yourself more clever than
> the cat, or the old woman? I will say nothing of
> myself. Don't imagine such nonsense, child, and
> thank your good fortune that you have been
> received here. Are you not in a warm room, and in

society from which you may learn something? But you are a chatterer, and your company is not very agreeable. Believe me, I speak only for your own good. I may tell you unpleasant truths, but that is a proof of my friendship. I advise you, therefore, to lay eggs, and learn to purr as quickly as possible (Andersen, "The Ugly Duckling").

Faced with these impossible demands, the ugly duckling decides to leave:

"I believe I must go out into the world again," said the duckling.

Everywhere he goes, he is rejected by those he meets because he is so "ugly." He cannot find any place where he is welcomed for who he is. The ugly duckling goes on his journey, not because he chooses it, but because he wants to escape the name-calling and the rejection. He wants to find a place where he can be at home.

The Ugly Duckling's Vision

The ugly duckling's unhappy journey continues. Now it is autumn. The cold weather begins. Then he sees something he has never seen before:

One evening, just as the sun set amid radiant clouds, there came a large flock of beautiful birds out of the bushes. The duckling had never seen any like them before. They were swans, and they curved their graceful necks, while their soft plumage shone with dazzling whiteness. They uttered a singular cry, as they spread their glorious wings and flew away from those cold regions to warmer countries across the sea.

As they mounted higher and higher in the air, the ugly little duckling felt quite a strange sensation as

> he watched them. He whirled himself in the water like a wheel, stretched out his neck towards them, and uttered a cry so strange that it frightened himself. Could he ever forget those beautiful, happy birds; and when at last they were out of his sight, he dived under the water, and rose again almost beside himself with excitement. He knew not the names of these birds, nor where they had flown, but he felt towards them as he had never felt for any other bird in the world. He was not envious of these beautiful creatures, but wished to be as lovely as they. Poor ugly creature, how gladly he would have lived even with the ducks had they only given him encouragement (Andersen, "The Ugly Duckling").

The young swan who thinks he is an ugly duckling sees swans flying overhead and feels something within him. He wants to be as lovely as the swans are. He still doesn't know that he already has that potential within him.

Even in the midst of his misery and the endless rejection he encounters, the young swan who thinks he is a duck has a vision of what he truly wants to become. This is the power of vision, those moments when you see something you have not seen before and you feel something within that you can't quite identify. But it touches you and won't let you go.

A Transformative Picture

I had such a vision when I was seven years old in the second grade. My vision took the form of a color illustration in our reading book. The central characters were Alice and Jerry and their little dog, Jip.

As I remember the picture, Alice and Jerry were running with outstretched arms toward their father who had just come home from work. Even Jip was running eagerly toward him. The picture showed their father from behind. His arms were opened wide, ready to receive his children as they ran to him.

That picture was a moment of revelation for me. I saw something I could not have imagined before—children who were glad to see their father come home. I couldn't imagine ever being glad to see my father come home. When he came home, I did my best to disappear. It was easier to hide outside. Inside the tiny house we lived in, there was nowhere to go, except to flatten myself against a wall as far out of his way as possible but I couldn't ever get far enough away.

He would cross the room, haul off with his left arm and hit me hard, spewing profanity as he bellowed, "Get the hell out of my way." No, I was never glad to see my father come home. But Alice and Jerry were glad to see their father and he was glad to see them.

I remember that picture as the first time in my life when I saw a different possibility for my life. I studied that picture as often as I could pull the book out of the desk and peek at the picture without being seen by the strict teacher with her rigid rules. She would punish a child for looking at a reading book anywhere except in the reading circle, under her militant supervision.

That picture showed me a vision of life in which people were actually glad to see each other come home. A plan formed in my mind. It was a simple plan. When I get old enough, I'm going to leave this place and never come back. I want to go where people are glad to see each other come home.

It took me until the age of twelve—and another moment of vision—until I grasped that what I was after was not a matter of geography but of decision.

For all its limitations, the decision I made at the age of seven was the first real turning point of my life. Even then, I knew that the unhappiness in that house was caused by too much alcohol and not enough food, too much violence and not enough tenderness, too much abuse and not enough love. I knew that my salvation from my tormenters meant running away from that place. That decision was the beginning of my own journey, just as the ugly duckling's journey began when he decided that he would leave the barnyard where he was treated so cruelly.

We'll leave the unhappy ugly duckling for now, with the promise to return to the point at the end of his journey when he realizes the truth about his identity. That is the moment when he knows his true self identity and is happy for the first time in his life.

Why Ugly Ducklings Leave Churches

People do not run away from places they feel safe, loved, and wanted. They run away because they are unloved, unsafe, and unwanted. People leave Christian churches for the same reasons. But even then, churches rarely consider why anyone would leave an environment that can't do any better than call people ugly ducklings who have to be "saved" from their innate ugliness, or in theological terms, "sinners who have to saved from their sinful natures."

The truth about the ugly duckling is that he isn't a duck. He is a swan. The truth about you is that you were not born a "sinner" and you don't have to be "saved" from your sinful self. You are already your true self, even if you don't know it yet.

This is a book for ugly ducklings who are still trapped in the Christian salvation trap, but have not yet found the mirror to show them their true identity.

I invite you to join me on the journey to set your true self free from the Christian salvation trap and to claim your perfect true self identity.

Part One

Original Sin

and

Your Identity

Chapter 1
Are You Living
Under a False Identity?

Know Yourself
Inscription At Delphi

Who Are You?

Who are you? Before you answer too quickly, ponder deeply. How you answer this question has everything to do with how you live your life.

The wisest words ever spoken in human history are the words from the ancient Temple of Apollo at Delphi, "know yourself."

But what if you really don't know yourself? What if what you believe to be true about your identity is actually false?

In his book, *Subliminal Persuasion*, Dave Lakhani refers briefly to his experience as an undercover narcotics officer when he helped people create new identities (Lakhani 47). Although it's a passing reference in a chapter intended to help people create effective marketing stories about their businesses, this little reference provides a powerful insight into how it's possible for you to live your life without knowing your true identity.

Although Lakhani makes only a brief allusion, I assume that he was working with people who were in a witness protection program because they knew too much. To keep them safe from retaliation and harm, they needed new identities. Those new identities were assumed identities, based on false names, false backstories, and false cover stories.

I'll return to Lakhani later for what he has to say about subliminal persuasion and belief, but for now, the relevant points contained within this passing reference is that stories create our identities and small changes in our stories are enough to create false identities.

Salvation Stories and Your Identity

The purpose of this book is to show you that much of what the Christian church claims to be true about your identity originated in various religious and philosophical beliefs in the Greco-Roman world rather than the Bible. This means that many "biblical" beliefs in the Christian church cannot be justified by the Bible itself.

The underlying premise of *Your True Self Identity* is that the dominant salvation story of the Christian church creates powerful identity stories for Christian believers that are actually *false identities* based on beliefs that did not come from the Bible. These false identities are the hidden cause of much of the struggle, suffering, and unhappiness in the lives of people affected by Christian salvation teaching. In the guise of forgiving believers from sin, these false identity stories trap believers into relentless shame.

The critical difference between the identity stories of people in witness protection programs and the identity stories of people in the Christian church is awareness of whether or not the identity stories are true. People in witness protection programs know their true identities and they know that their assumed identities are false.

In contrast, many people in Christian churches don't know the truth about their identities. This means that many believers actually live their lives with assumed identities, based on false stories about themselves, and never know their true identities. They live in an *identity concealment program* that hides their true identities from them.

And this leads me back to your identity. What if you are living your life with a false identity and you don't even know it? This question is the most important question you can ask and the most important question you can answer, because every other belief about your identity depends on how you answer the question, Who are you?

Did Someone Create a False Identity for You?

What if much of the struggle, suffering, and unhappiness of your life are direct results of a false story that hides your true identity? Imagine that there was someone in your life who created a false identity for you at your birth, an identity that kept you trapped in guilt and shame and fear.

Does this seem farfetched? Actually, if you were born into the Christian church, there was someone who did exactly that. He was Saint Augustine. He set in motion a process more than sixteen hundred years ago to create false identities for Christian believers by formulating the doctrine of original sin. This is certainly not the way that Christian history regards Augustine. However, this is the essence of Augustine's impact on Christian identities.

He created a new identity for every human being by changing biblical creation stories to create a new story. This new story identifies every human being as a sinner because of original sin. The doctrine of original sin becomes the foundation for your false identity story. The new story not only hides your true identity from the world, it also hides your true identity from you. This is the false identity that can trap Christian believers into helplessness, guilt, and shame. The result is the *salvation trap*. My purpose is to show you where the salvation trap came from and how you can set yourself free from it.

How did this doctrine of original sin develop? Just as biblical books are products of their own religious, political, social, historical, geographical, linguistic, and personal contexts, theological doctrines do not drop out of the sky fully formed. Theological doctrines are also products of their own religious, political, social, historical, geographical, linguistic, theological, and personal contexts.

In other words, theological doctrines are always created in particular times and places, by particular people, to respond to particular circumstances, to answer particular questions.

And so, rather than consider the doctrine of original sin as an abstract theological doctrine, we need to go beyond the abstractions to find the personal story behind it.

The Inner Questions of Augustine's Story

The doctrine of original sin emerged from the personal story of Saint Augustine, the Bishop of Hippo, in what is now Algeria, in North Africa. He lived from 354 to 430, in the era of "the church fathers."

Every life story comprises outer circumstances and inner questions. Rather than start with the outer circumstances of Augustine's life in a time and place of religious conflict and religious synthesis, let's begin with his compelling inner questions.

Theologies are deeply personal efforts to answer the most compelling questions of human life. Who am I? What is life about? What does my life mean? Why do bad things happen to me? If God exists, why do I suffer? Why? Why? Why?

Augustine's *Confessions*

Augustine was a prolific writer who produced a multitude of theological books. The one that reveals his deepest personal questions is his *Confessions*. Augustine wrote the

Confessions at age 43, while he was serving as Bishop of Hippo.

I want to make clear that I am a biblical scholar rather than an Augustine scholar or a theologian. I have read Augustine's *Confessions* only in English translations, rather than in the Latin original. To compensate somewhat for relying on translations, I include citations from two translations rather than one. These translations are by Maria Boulding and Albert C. Outler.

There are many ways to read Augustine's *Confessions.* One way is to read it theologically, to understand how Augustine defines Christian belief about God, human nature, sin, and salvation. Another way is to read it as a classic of Christian spiritual literature by one of the most influential figures in the history of the Christian church.

For me, *The Confessions* is almost too painful to read. Whatever anyone can say about this autobiographical writing as a classic of religious literature, I see it as a legacy of the enduring effects of childhood abuse on a vulnerable child. Augustine describes a lifetime of grief, guilt, and shame experienced by an unhappy man who never experienced assurance of his own salvation.

In his *Confessions*, Augustine writes about the severe beatings he received from his teachers when he first went away to school at the age of eleven. What he says about the beatings, coming so close to the beginning of his book, is a crucial insight into the brokenhearted and tormented man who wrote *The Confessions.* Even more significantly, Augustine's narrative about the beatings demonstrates why the Christian church creates so many wounded people in the name of salvation.

Augustine's Identity of Shame

Augustine's life story is a story of shame masquerading as a story of guilt. Although guilt and shame are often treated as synonyms, shame is a very different experience than guilt. Feelings of guilt come from remorse about actions you take or don't take. Feelings of shame come from your own sense of your identity. In other words, guilt is about what you do. Shame is about who you are. At its core, shame is a deep sense of self-deficiency. You feel that something is seriously wrong with you.

Donald Capps, in *The Depleted Self*, connects shame with "an unmet hunger for admiration and approval" (Capps 39). Augustine's story reveals his relentless torment about his belief that something essential is wrong with him as well as his endless desire for approval. Such shame cannot be healed by confession of guilt.

Here, I will comment only on the first few pages of the *Confessions* rather than attempt to give an overview of the whole book. Regrettably, these first few pages are enough to describe the whole. If you understand how he thinks here, you can understand how he thinks throughout the book. This is a story of someone who is deeply tormented by shame about himself.

Augustine's *Confessions* begins with this paragraph:

> Great are you, O Lord, and exceedingly worthy of praise, your power is immense, and your wisdom is beyond reckoning. And so we humans who are a due part of your creation, long to praise you—we who carry our mortality about with us, carry the evidence of our sin and with it the proof that you thwart the proud (Boulding 3).

These two sentences are packed with allusions to scripture. They are also packed with meaning. Augustine refers to the "Lord" and then he refers to "humans." What he says about "humans" in this sentence conveys the essence of Augustine's belief about what it is to be human. It also conveys the reason why God "thwarts" human beings. (Instead of "thwart," Outler translates the verb as "resist.")

What Augustine Says about God

Before we get to what Augustine says about human beings as born sinners, it's even more important to see what Augustine is saying about God. For Augustine, God is unresponsive to human efforts to please God.

Augustine asserts that humans desire to praise God, but because humans are mortal, even the desire to praise God is evidence of sin. Mortality is not only evidence of sin, it is proof that God "thwarts" or "resists" the proud.

In some respects, you don't have to read any more to understand why Augustine's *Confessions* is the written record of a tormented man. The torment and the justification for the torment are here, encapsulated in two sentences.

Longing to Praise God

After these two sentences, Augustine continues with these words. I include the translations by both Boulding and Outler here, because this passage contains what are probably the most well-known words from Augustine's *Confessions:*

> Yet these humans, due part of your creation as they are, still do long to praise you. You arouse us so that praising you may bring us joy, because you have made us and drawn us to yourself, and our heart is unquiet until it rests in you (Boulding 3).

> Still he desires to praise you, this man who is only a small part of your creation. You have prompted him, that he should delight to praise you, for you have made us for yourself and restless is our heart until it comes to rest in you (Outler 3).

Let's look at this carefully. Augustine is saying here that humans long to praise God. Why? Because God puts the desire into human nature. Then he includes this claim, which I first heard translated this way:

> You have made us for yourself, O Lord, and our
> hearts are restless until they rest in you.

These words are foundational in Christian spirituality. When I first heard this reference, as a student in theological seminary, the professor spoke eloquently about how these words convey the longing within each human being to come home to God. At that point, I had not yet read Augustine's *Confessions*. I certainly did not understand how much Augustine's theology was deeply influenced by Manichaean beliefs that spirit is good and matter is evil.

I'm quite sure that I understood it the way the professor intended. If we are restless, it is because we have turned away from God in our sinfulness. God is willing, but humans—proud sinners that we are—are unwilling to accept God's invitation to find rest in God.

However, in the context of Augustine's *Confessions*, Augustine's words—however they are translated—convey a much less comforting meaning. Augustine's words remind me of something else.

How to Break an Eager Spirit

During my husband's service as an officer in the United States Air Force, we stayed with another officer and his wife for two or three days while we were waiting for our base housing unit to be available.

They had recently acquired a puppy. The puppy was the living embodiment of the tail-wagging, eager-to-please canine nature that wants nothing more than to please and to receive love and praise in return. Too bad for that puppy that Tom did not return love and praise for the eager efforts of the puppy to please him. Instead, Tom tormented the puppy with endless teasing.

One of Tom's little games involved hiding food from the puppy. He would fill a dish with food, hold it under the puppy's nose. Then he hid the dish inside the cabinet under the sink. Then the little dog went nuts trying to get at the food. Then Tom would open the cabinet door just enough for the puppy to see the food. But before the puppy could get at the dish, Tom shut the door. Tom did this several times, before he let the puppy have the food. Tom took the best in the puppy's nature—his innate canine sense of loyalty—and used it to betray that loyalty again and again.

Some time after that, we had some reason to visit them again—it surely wasn't because we desired their company. By then, Tom had turned an eager, tail-wagging puppy into a whimpering, cowering, broken-spirited little dog. During our visit, we heard indignant complaints about the neighbors who called in reports about the little dog tied outside without shelter or water for hours in the oppressive, humid heat of an Arkansas summer. Tom considered it no one's business except his own how he treated his dog.

When I read Saint Augustine's *Confessions*, I do not see the words of a great theologian who has uplifting words that will elevate Christian believers into a relationship of love and trust with God. Instead, I see the words of someone whose spirit was broken just as the spirit of that little puppy was broken. Someone who spends a lifetime trying to please God but gets only torment in return from a distant and capricious master.

Tied Up in Knots

Augustine follows these words with a series of questions about what he is supposed to do to praise God correctly. In other words, Augustine begins the process of tying himself into theological knots. He asks if he should invoke God or praise God. But then he wants to know how he can invoke

God if he doesn't know God first. And then he wants to know if he can call on God. He goes on from these questions to other questions. How can you call on one you don't know? And how you call on someone if you don't believe? And how can you believe if you don't have a preacher?

In all of this, Augustine reminds me of people getting themselves into a stew over possibilities. Imagine someone who hears a weather forecast about a big rainstorm on the way and then begins a breathless cascade of "what ifs."

What if it rains so hard that the roof leaks and what if the living room carpet gets wet and what if I have to replace the carpet but I won't be able to afford it if I have to get the roof fixed and what if I have to fix the roof and I won't be able to pay the electric bill and what if I won't have any electricity and what if I don't have any electricity and what if I oversleep because my clock radio won't work without electricity and so I get to work late and what if I get fired from my job and....and... and...

It's not that I don't know how to tie myself in knots. I can do it very well. Maybe you're good at it too. All it takes is to start with one "what if" and never stop until you reach a level of worry that immobilizes you with helplessness. This kind of cascade into helplessness is not the way of a hero. It is the way of a victim. It leads to nowhere except a swamp of misery that gets deeper and deeper.

Who Will Help Me Find Peace?

At this point, Augustine has barely begun his cascade of possibilities...and we're still on the first page of the *Confessions*. But he goes on and on, with other paragraphs filled with such questions, until he gets to what he wants most of all:

> Who shall bring me to rest in you? Who will send you
> into my heart so to overwhelm it that my sins shall

be blotted out and I may embrace you, my only good?

...

So speak that I may hear. Behold, the ears of my heart are before you, lord; open them and say to my soul, I am your salvation. I will hasten after that voice, and I will lay hold upon you. Hide not your face from me. Even if I die, let me see your face lest I die (Outler 5).

I read these words as the poignant longing of a tormented person who wants nothing more than to find rest in God. He longs for salvation. He wants God to save him from his sins. More than that, I read these words as someone who wants to be at peace. He wants to rest in God, but he is never sure that he will ever find rest, because he is never sure that he is getting it right. He pleads that God will not hide from him.

The longings expressed here shape the rest of Augustine's *Confessions*. He wants peace...but he can never find it...because he can never be sure that he is getting it right...because he is a sinner...therefore God hides from him. This is a recipe for unhappiness, confusion, and torment.

As a biblical scholar who has studied the Hebraic creation stories in Genesis deeply, I can also tell you that this kind of torment has almost nothing to do with Hebraic creation traditions about the nature of God and God's promises toward human beings. It also has almost nothing to do with anything found in New Testament Gospel stories.

How Augustine Took Revenge on His Elders

Augustine goes on, in these first few pages of his *Confessions*, to describe his infancy. Although he makes clear that he doesn't remember any of it, he bases his claims on his observations of babies and young children. The tangled reasoning of these paragraphs makes clear why he can never get what he seeks in this life.

He describes his experience as a very young child who wants something but doesn't have the capacity to get what he wants. And so, he does what babies and small children do. He flails his arms and legs, doing what he can to get someone to meet his needs.

But no one gives him what he wants. Why? Because baby Augustine didn't make himself clear enough or because it wouldn't be good for him to have what he wanted. It never enters his explanation that the adults in his world didn't provide what he needed. No, it's all his fault. He blames himself. He wanted to "rule his elders." He wanted them to "serve him as slaves." And because he didn't get what he wanted, "...I would take revenge on them by bursting into tears" (Boulding 7).

The characterization of crying as taking "revenge" because he wanted his elders to be his "slaves" is a clue that crying is an important theme in Augustine's life. It's also a clue to Augustine's attitude toward children. In all of this, the story that Augustine tells about his life puts all the blame on his sinful nature and exonerates the adults responsible for his care.

What is most important to recognize is that all of this heavy guilt is being laid upon a crying baby who did what babies do. He cried because he wanted something he was unable to provide for himself.

The themes laid out in these few paragraphs are the themes of Augustine's life story. No matter what he wants, he is not going to get it. No one is going to help him, because he is a sinner...especially not God.

Going Away to School

After his imaginings about his infancy, Augustine begins with the first remembered episode of his life. Beginnings are always significant because beginnings set stories in motion. And beginning stories set lives in motion.

He describes his experience of being sent away from home to go to school when he was eleven. He begins this way:

> God, my god! What miseries and mockeries did I then experience when it was impressed on me that obedience to my teachers was proper to my boyhood estate if I was to flourish in this world and distinguish myself in those tricks of speech which would gain honor for me among men, and deceitful riches! To this end I was sent to school to get learning, the value of which I knew not—wretch that I was.

> Yet if I was slow to learn, I was flogged. For this was deemed praiseworthy by our forefathers and many had passed before us in the same course, and thus had built up the precedent for the sorrowful road on which we too were compelled to travel, multiplying labor and sorrow upon the sons of Adam (Outler 9).

In other words, Augustine was sent away to school against his own wishes. When he didn't study his lessons enough, he was beaten by his teachers. Augustine laments that this kind of physical punishment for errant students was just the way it was, the way it had always been, demonstrating that human life on Earth is full of work and sorrow.

Augustine Prays for Salvation from the Beatings

Augustine follows these words with this significant passage:

> About this time, lord, I observed men calling upon you, and learned from them to conceive you—after my capacity for understanding as it was then—to be some great being, who, though not visible to our senses, was able to hear and help us. Thus as a boy I began to call upon you, my help and my refuge, and in calling you, broke the bands of my tongue. Small as I was, I prayed with no slight earnestness that I might not be beaten at school. And when you did not heed me—for that would have been giving me over to my folly—my elders and even my parents too, who wished me no ill, treated my stripes as a joke, though they were then a great and grievous ill to me (Outler 9-10).

Augustine says that he first learned about God and prayer and heard that God both hears and helps those who ask for help. And so for the first time in his life, he began to pray. He prayed that he would not be beaten at school. How did God answer his earnest prayers? God did not answer. Augustine also says that his parents laughed at him. No one stopped the beatings.

The Emotional Truth of Augustine's Story

Although it's presumptuous to psychoanalyze any historical figure, we can get to the emotional truth behind the story that Augustine tells us about his identity.

Augustine was an abused child who asked for help and didn't get it from anyone. He didn't get help from the teachers who beat him. He didn't get help from his parents who laughed at him and sent him back to the school. And he certainly didn't get help from the God who was deaf to his prayers to be saved from the beatings. This is the story that forms his identity.

From this beginning, Augustine went on to develop the doctrine of original sin.

The Essential Wound

One of my writing teachers, Hal Zina Bennett, refers to what he calls an "essential wound" (Bennett 109). An essential wound is some experience that is so traumatic that it creates an enduring wound that affects your *essence*—your true self. Bennett makes clear that the enduring wound is not the event itself, but the response to your experience of the traumatic event by the people you trust and love. Will they believe you? Will they take your suffering seriously? Will they help you? Will they call you a liar when you tell the truth? Will they laugh at you? Or will they ignore you and let you suffer?

From my perspective, Augustine's essential wound was not the beatings, but the lack of concern by God and his parents to the beatings. God did not answer his prayers to stop the beatings and his parents did not stop the beatings. His parents laughed and God didn't answer. This experience was the essential wound that shaped Augustine's life and his theology.

As far as I can discern, Augustine's theology is the result of this essential wound. Who was God for Augustine? The God who can hear and help but doesn't answer and doesn't help. The God who hides his face from Augustine who wanted nothing more than to see God's face. Why does God hide? Because Augustine is a sinner.

Indifferent to Torture

What happens next in Augustine's narrative is critical to the role of original sin in the theology of the Christian church.

In a particularly poignant section, he wonders how anyone who claims to love God can be indifferent to the pleas of tortured people to be spared from torture and to scorn anyone who is afraid of being tortured. Then he compares torture to the punishments inflicted on the boys by their teachers. He wonders how the parents of the boys could be amused by the torments inflicted on the boys.

And after all of this, he lets God off the hook:

> For we were no less afraid of our pains, nor did we beseech you less to escape them. Yet, even so, we were sinning by writing or reading or studying less than our assigned lessons (Outler 10).

He goes on to develop the reason why he deserved the beatings. He wanted to play ball instead of study. Augustine "sinned" because he was not obedient to his parents and his teachers. Because he was disobedient to authority, God would not save him from the beatings.

Augustine's Story

Augustine's story of misery follows a particular structure. It goes something like this:

- Poor me. I had to do something because someone else made me do it.

- The thing I had to do was worthless, all for vanity and money and pride.

- But I had no choice, so I did it.

- But I never did it well enough. So I was punished for disobedience.

- Then I prayed to you, God, asking you to save me from this thing I didn't want to do.

- But you didn't answer me, because I was supposed to be obedient to authority and do it anyway, even though it was worthless, all for vanity and money and pride.

- You were right to ignore me and make me endure this misery, because I am a worthless sinner and everything I do is wrong anyway.

How Augustine's Essential Wound Becomes His Theology

Am I being unfair to one of the greatest saints of the Christian church? Beyond any sense of compassion I have for the pain I read on every page of Augustine's *Confessions*, I see all too clearly how much Augustine's doctrine of original sin has inflicted enormous suffering on generations of innocent people.

We can't know what might have been, but it is possible to see how Augustine's essential wound shapes his identity story.

We see it in his opening words when he describes a distant God who creates people with the desire to praise God, but then doesn't answer, because the ones who call upon God are proud sinners. We see it in his description of his infancy, when he describes the cries of a helpless baby as the demands of a little tyrant who wants to turn the adults around him into slaves. This description makes the baby the one who is guilty and makes the adults right to ignore his cries.

Throughout the rest of his sad story, he follows the same template. He describes the misery of an experience, because someone did something to him, but he ends up by calling himself a sinner and says that God is right to let him suffer, because Augustine has been disobedient in some way. The effect of Augustine's essential wound is evident throughout his *Confessions*.

It is nowhere more evident than in how he treats his own son, Adeodatus. In one notable example, Augustine would not allow either himself or his son to cry when Augustine's mother died, because crying would demonstrate lack of faith in God.

What If?

As a child who never had anyone save me from my own hellish childhood, I read Augustine's story and I ask these *what if?* questions. What if his teachers didn't beat their students? What if Augustine's parents didn't laugh at him when he told them about the beatings? What if Augustine's parents had taken their son out of that school? What if Augustine believed that God had answered his prayers because the beatings stopped?

Later, we'll come to what the Gospel of Mathew has to say about the abuse of *little ones*. In Matthew, Jesus never lets anyone off the hook for abusing little ones. What if Augustine had grasped what Jesus says in the Gospel of Matthew about the abuse of the vulnerable?

I think that it could have transformed the world. It would certainly have transformed the church. Can you imagine a church that was less concerned with teaching children to be obedient to authority—even abusive authority—and more concerned about not breaking the spirits of children and little ones who don't have enough power to defend themselves?

Chapter 2
The Doctrine of Original Sin
And Your Identity

Man is the only kind of varmint sets his
own trap, baits it, and then steps in it.
John Steinbeck

Guilty of Inherited Sin

Augustine's doctrine of original sin claims that your true identity is that you are a sinner. He makes this claim based on the biblical story of Adam and Eve in Genesis 2-3.

In fact, Augustine's ideas about original sin owe far more to his exposure to Latin philosophy and literature, Greek rhetoric, and Hellenistic religions—particularly Manichaeism—than it does to Hebraic theological traditions. He has in fact distorted the story of Adam and Eve in significant ways. Regrettably, Augustine's distortions of this biblical creation story frequently define the stories the Christian church tells about "Adam and Eve," "original sin," "the fall of man," and your identity as a human being.

Let's begin with the idea of "original sin." In the identity story Augustine created for you, you were born guilty of sin. You might ask: How could I be guilty of anything when I was born? Augustine's answer is: You "inherited your guilt from Adam." You are guilty of sin because Adam sinned by disobeying God. You must pay the price.

According to Augustine, Adam's sin is coded into your essence the way your inherited DNA determines the color of your eyes—and you can't do anything to change either one.

Theologians have found much in this doctrine to challenge. In fact, theologians who were Augustine's contemporaries argued with Augustine himself about this idea. Theologians have argued about this idea for the last sixteen hundred years. They are still arguing about it. Here, I will make no attempt to sort through the doctrine of original sin as theology.

Why the Doctrine of Original Sin Creates False Identities

My focus is on the story itself as it functions to create identity. My claim is that the doctrine of original sin creates false identities in Christian believers. If you believe you are what Augustine's doctrine of original sin claims about you, you will live your life under an assumed identity that hides your true identity from the world and from yourself. You will believe that you are a sinner who was born guilty of someone else's sin and you will believe that you are powerless to change your identity as a sinner.

But isn't this what the Bible claims about you? Doesn't the Bible say this in Genesis when it tells the story of how Adam and Eve were kicked out the Garden of Eden because of their disobedience to God? Doesn't the Bible refer to the "fall" when humanity fell into sin? Doesn't the Bible say that Jesus came to save human beings from Adam's sin? Doesn't the Bible say that Jesus had to die on the cross to atone for Adam's guilt?

No, it really doesn't. Much of this *common knowledge* about the Bible and "the fall of man" and "Adam's sin," and "original sin," and how "Jesus died on the cross to pay the price to redeem sinful humanity from guilt for Adam's sin," results from distortions of Bible stories.

The Doctrine of Original Sin as a Filter for the Bible

Augustine's doctrine of original sin has become a powerful filter for the Bible itself. All filters let some components pass through a filtering medium while it blocks other components. The filtered result is not the same as the original.

The doctrine of original sin is a powerful filter that turns the innocent into sinners, just as original sin holds newborn babies—who haven't had time to commit their own sins—guilty for Adam's sin.

But how did this doctrine of original sin develop? Augustine wasn't the first theologian to use the phrase, "original sin." The phrase itself goes back to the second century *church father* Tertullian, but Augustine is the church father who created the doctrine that has shaped the church.

Three Components

In simplest terms, Augustine's doctrine of original sin has three essential components:

- Original sin originated when Adam and Eve freely chose to disobey God by eating the fruit of "the tree of the knowledge of good and evil."

- All subsequent generations inherit the guilt for this sin.

- Original sin is fundamentally about sexual desire.

Let's look at these three components one at a time.

Genesis 2-3 as History

First, the doctrine of original sin treats the creation story in Genesis 2-3 as historical fact. It claims that Adam and Eve were the first human beings and that they disobeyed God by eating the fruit of the tree. This disobedience to God's command was the "original sin." Before Adam and Eve, there was no sin in the world.

Born Guilty of Adam's Sin

Second, all human beings are born guilty of this original sin. This guilt is based on Augustine's claim that the whole human race existed in Adam as one organic unity at the time of his disobedience. Therefore, human beings don't just inherit the tendency to sin, we are born *guilty* of Adam's sin.

Original Sin and Sexual Desire

The third critical component of Augustine's formulation of original sin is the idea of "concupiscence." This fancy theological language is a way of saying that sexual desire is directly involved in original sin because it distorts human will. Concupiscence is strong sexual desire that overcomes the will to obey God.

The Seeds of the Fathers

It's worth noting in passing here that most theological formulations of original sin refer to "Adam's sin." You might wonder about Eve's role in all of this. Does the human race inherit "original sin" from her? This theological formulation is a clue to something that many modern readers might miss.

This Augustinian language about "Adam's sin" reflects the dominant understanding of human reproduction in the ancient world. The ancients had no understanding of genetics and DNA. They didn't know what modern science has taught us, that each of us gets half of our genes from our mothers and half from our fathers. The ancient world understood that only fathers transmit human essence in the form of preformed individuals—the *homunculus* (Latin for "little human"). In metaphorical terms, fathers plant *seeds* that contain fully-formed little humans.

In contrast to fathers, mothers contribute nothing of essence. Mothers only provide places for the seeds to grow. This means that Adam already contained the whole of humanity in his "seed." This is how the guilt of Adam is transmitted to all subsequent generations.

Misbegotten Males

I also note in passing that this claim also means that each little *homunculus* is male because he was formed from the essence of his father. As you can imagine, this created a bit of a problem for the explanation when about half of the little males turned out to be little females.

Even such a formidable intellect as Aristotle had to go to rather absurd lengths to maintain the validity of the claim about fathers planting little male *homunculus* seeds. Aristotle speculated about the effect of the wind on pregnant women. He also wondered about the effect of sour milk on mothers-to-be. These are two of the possibilities he offered to explain how so many little males could be born as little females.

The conclusion of his argument is that a female is a defective human. Or as Aristotle put it, a "misbegotten male," the product of some sort of accident to the *homunculus* seed after it was "planted."

It's all rather hilarious until you stop and consider how much this erroneous belief has devalued females as less than fully human for more than two thousand years. But that's not the story I am telling right now, so I will leave it and get back to Augustine.

Augustine's story has devalued all of us for most of Christian history. Augustine's doctrine of original sin declares that all of us—male and female alike—are beings who were born defective because we were born guilty of inherited sin.

Original Sin in the Twenty-First Century

Before we go any further into how this doctrine of original sin emerged from Augustine's own life experiences and his own personal questions, you can see that this doctrine rests on shaky ground, especially for people living in the twenty-first century.

Among other leaps of logic, it requires us to take Genesis as factual history. It requires us to forget what we know about biology. It also requires us to abandon a foundational principle of modern law—you are guilty only for your own crimes. You are not guilty for crimes done by other people, especially not ancient ancestors.

This doctrine also raises all sorts of questions about the connection between free will and obedience to God. And significantly, it also requires us all to feel very, very guilty about sex.

Although theologians have been arguing about Augustine's formulation of original sin since the days of Augustine himself, on every point imaginable, all discussions of these topics somehow have to accept, rebut, or refine Augustine's statements about original sin.

Chapter 3
Augustine's Search for Identity

The heresy of one age becomes the
orthodoxy of the next.

Helen Keller

Augustine's Biography

The previous chapter introduced Augustine as he
introduced himself in his *Confessions*—a tormented man
whose theology was set in motion by his experience of being
beaten by his teachers when he was a child at school.
Augustine experienced the essential wound that defined his
theology when he prayed to God to stop the beatings and
God did not save him. This part of the story is left out of
many descriptions of Augustine's life story.

With that life-defining essential wound in mind, we can
now get to the biographical details of Augustine's life. The
major source of information about Augustine comes from
his own writings, including his autobiographical writing,
the *Confessions*. I make no effort to sort out historical fact
from fiction in Augustine's story. Instead, my focus is on
the story that Augustine tells about himself.

Augustine was born in the fourth century of the
Christian era. This was a crucial time in the history of the
church, filled with intense controversies over theological
orthodoxy.

These controversies also included disputes over which
writings were "orthodox" and which were "heretical." The
early centuries of the Christian church produced a flood of

writings with widely divergent claims about the nature of Jesus and the meaning of Christian faith.

In short, it was an era much like our own. It was a time when various religious and philosophical traditions and cultures were colliding, confronting, and colluding with each other. Such eras produce new doctrines and new understandings of ancient religions as they encounter new religions. The inevitable result of such ferment is that old religions get reinterpreted to create new religions. These new religions are syntheses between old and new.

Defining Orthodox Christian Belief

The critical point is that this era was pivotal for determining orthodoxy in the Christian church. Augustine was very much part of the effort to declare what is orthodox Christian belief and what is heresy.

Augustine's birth in 354 was only 29 years after what church history calls "The First Council of Nicea." If you have ever recited "the Nicene Creed" in church, this council was the source of that creed.

The traditional story is that the council was called in 325 by Emperor Constantine to establish the orthodox creed of the church. The hot issue was what it declared the "Arian heresy" that Christ was created by God and not entirely identical to God.

The Council of Nicea is also credited with deciding the orthodox canon of scripture, which also meant that it decided which writings were excluded from the orthodox canon. The list of books that make up the Bible in our era was more or less settled by the Council of Nicea. Notice the "more or less" here.

How and when and where the Christian church, in both the West and the East, determined what was orthodox and what was heretical was a long, complicated, messy, and deeply political process. Trying to figure out what really happened is enough to make your head spin.

Augustine's "Mixed" Background

Augustine was part of that complicated and messy process of defining orthodox Christian belief. His life story demonstrates a conflicting mix of religious beliefs and personal identity challenges. The comment by his contemporary, Saint Jerome—the translator of the Bible into Latin (the *Vulgate*)—is very significant. According to Jerome, Augustine "established anew the ancient faith" (*conditor antiquae rursum fidei*).

Augustine's effort to establish anew the ancient faith was a process of synthesis. If you look at his life story, you can see why. Few people in the history of the church had more conflicting life elements to put together.

Augustine was born to a pagan father, Patricius (a name that means *father* in Latin) and a Christian mother, Monica. His North African ancestors gained legal status as Roman citizens at least a century before Augustine was born. This means that Augustine was a Latin-speaking North African with Roman citizenship, in a family with a built-in potential for religious conflict, who grew up in an area that was predominantly pagan. These details are only the beginning features of a life filled with potential for conflict between opposing options.

More simply put, Augustine faced the challenge of people of "mixed" background. He had to figure out how to put these pieces together. From a psychological perspective, the story of Augustine looks like a quest to figure out who he was and where he belonged.

Am I a Banana?

I remember long conversations with a teaching colleague who was born in San Francisco's Chinatown to illegal immigrants from China. That meant he was a legal citizen but his parents were not. Throughout his childhood, the family lived under an assumed name, under the constant fear that they would be caught by immigration authorities, and his parents and Chinese-born older brother would be deported back to China. His first language was a dialect of Cantonese. He learned English in school but his parents never learned to speak the language. He became a Christian as a young child through a Christian outreach program in Chinatown. Eventually, he was ordained into Christian ministry.

My friend sometimes spoke about the ongoing question of his life: Who am I? He wondered out loud if he was really a "banana"—yellow on the outside and white on the inside. In one memorable moment of our long friendship, he once mused about whether he was "Chinese enough" while we were eating lunch together in Chinatown. On that day, he was enjoying what he said were his two favorite foods. My tongue-in-cheek response was that someone whose favorite foods are chicken feet and bitter melon probably doesn't have to worry about being Chinese enough. His concern over identity didn't end with himself. I once asked how his children from his marriage to a white woman identified themselves. He said they considered themselves Chinese.

These are the identity questions of people who find themselves somehow "mixed." Who am I? Where do I belong? How do I put together the widely disparate components of my life into a whole identity?

Augustine's Journey from Here to There and Back Again

Augustine had the same challenges. As a young child, Augustine was reared as a Christian under his mother's influence. His family had enough wealth to send him away to school at the age of eleven, where he studied Latin literature as well as pagan beliefs and practices—all while enduring the beatings inflicted by his teachers. He returned home at the age of fifteen, where he studied Latin philosophy. At seventeen, he was sent to Carthage to study rhetoric. Study of Greek rhetoric is definitely not the ticket to success in our era, but it was the course of study that Patricius thought would put Augustine on the fast track to fame and fortune.

In Carthage, Augustine abandoned the Christian faith of his mother to become part of the Manichaean religion for about ten years. After Carthage, he went to Rome when he was twenty-nine to teach rhetoric. In Rome, he renounced Manichaeism. He then went to Milan where he studied Neo-Platonism. In Milan, he converted to Christianity and was baptized at Easter in 387. He then returned to North Africa and created a monastic order. In 391 he was ordained a priest and by 396 he became bishop of Hippo, at the age of 42. He was bishop of Hippo for thirty-four years until his death in 430, during the siege of Hippo by the Vandals.

The Influence of Manichaeism on Augustine

Augustine's story demonstrates that his early years were a religious seesaw between Christianity and other religious and philosophical ideas. The strongest influence was Manichaeism. Although he renounced Manichaeism and railed against it as a preacher and writer, Augustine was deeply influenced by Manichaean beliefs, which are evident in his notions about original sin.

Manichaeism originated in Persia in the third century, and was itself a synthesis of elements of Zoroastrianism, Buddhism, Christianity, and Gnosticism. It was a dualistic system of opposing forces of equal power. Think of the "light side" and the "dark side" of the Force in *Star Wars*. Spirit against matter. Good against evil. God against Satan. In this system, spirit is good and matter is evil. In a system in which matter is evil, sex is definitely evil. This dualistic worldview was enormously influential in the early centuries of the Christian church, from both Manichaeism and Gnosticism. Gnosticism was also an extremely powerful influence on the early Christian church.

After Augustine renounced Manichaeism, he condemned this dualistic worldview as heretical. However, his writings make clear that Augustine never quite got beyond Manichaeism ideas that spirit is good and matter is evil and sex is inherently sinful.

Sex and the Sinner Augustine

A strong theme of Augustine's story is his conflict about sex. Augustine went to Carthage at seventeen. From his description of his life in the *Confessions*, Augustine's life in Carthage resembled a college boy with raging hormones who was far away from home.

During his Manichaeism years in Carthage, Augustine fathered a son named Adeodatus with a woman who was to be with him for thirteen years. When modern writers mention this relationship, she is variously described as a mistress or a concubine or even a girlfriend. It is significant that no one—least of all Augustine in his writings—gives her a name. It is also significant that the sexual desire that was to become such an important component of Augustine's doctrine of original sin was very much a part of Augustine's life throughout much of his life. The most notable quotation to express his ongoing conflict about sexual desire is his prayer, "Make me chaste, but not yet."

Monica Dearest

Augustine's relationship with his mother, Monica, is an important part of his story. In conflicts of will with his mother, Augustine invariably lost. One incident is particularly relevant here. While Augustine was in Milan,

Monica arrived from North Africa and pressured Augustine to abandon the mother of his son and to send her back to North Africa, so that Monica could arrange a socially advantageous marriage for Augustine.

Augustine complied with his mother's wishes and sent the mother of his son back to North Africa. Adeodatus stayed with Augustine. Through Monica's efforts, Augustine was engaged to an eleven-year old girl. Since the girl was old enough to be engaged, but two years too young to marry, Augustine began a relationship with another young woman. Or as Augustine puts it in his *Confessions,* "I got myself another woman" (Boulding 118). The marriage never took place because Augustine broke the engagement. By his own account, Augustine was heartbroken over losing the woman he loved.

Pick Up and Read

During his years in Italy, Augustine went through several life-changing experiences, including a profound experience of hearing a voice telling him to "pick it up and read" and then reading these words from the Apostle Paul:

> Let us live honorably as in the day, not in reveling and drunkenness, not in debauchery and licentiousness, not in quarreling and jealousy. Instead, put on the Lord Jesus Christ, and make no provision for the flesh, to gratify its desires (Romans 13-13-14, NRSV).

Paul and Augustine As Synthesizers

Significantly, for someone who had prayed, "Lord, make me chaste, but not yet," the words that triggered his conversion to Christianity are words about the "desires of the flesh"— including sexual desire. Not surprisingly, these are words from the Apostle Paul, a man whose letters indicate that he had his own conflicts about sex and sexuality in Christian life.

The Apostle Paul was a Jew from Tarsus, in what is now modern day Turkey. He was a Roman citizen and a native Greek speaker, who took Christianity to the Greco-Roman world.

In many ways, Paul's life parallels Augustine's. Paul and Augustine were the most influential figures in the early centuries of the Christian church. Although Paul lived in the first century and Augustine was born in the fourth, they lived and worked in the Greco-Roman world shaped by religious and philosophical traditions rather than Hebraic traditions. Both were synthesizers, attempting to integrate the Hebraic origins of Christian faith into a world full of conflicting ideas, including ideas about sex.

Augustine Returns to Christianity

Augustine's conversion experience at the age of thirty-three led to his decisions to renounce his career as a rhetoric teacher and finally to be baptized as a Christian, much to the joy of his mother. And significantly, his conversion experience led Augustine to give up sex. Not long after his baptism, Monica died. Augustine vowed to live the rest of his life as a celibate priest.

In other words, Augustine returned to Christianity after considerable immersion in non-Christian religions, as well as Latin philosophy, literature, and Greek rhetoric, bearing deep grief, guilt, and lifelong shame, with a strong inclination to renounce sex to atone for his own sexual desires.

Original Sin and Hebrew Creation Stories

The Christian doctrine of original sin emerged from Augustine's life experiences. The doctrine of original sin has far more to do with Manichaean ideas about the body and sex than it has to do with anything in Hebraic traditions.

The only comment I will make here about the two creation stories in Genesis is that neither story treats matter and sexuality as inherently evil. Far from it. In the first Hebraic creation account in Genesis 1, God created human beings in God's image, blessed them, and told them to be fruitful and multiply:

> So God created humankind in his image, in the image of God he created them; male and female he created them. God blessed them, and God said to them, "Be fruitful and multiply, and fill the earth and subdue it; and have dominion over the fish of the sea and over the birds of the air and over every living thing that moves upon the earth" (Genesis 1:27-28, NRSV).

The connection between blessing and being fruitful and multiplying is a strong indication that sex itself is considered a blessing in Hebraic tradition.

In the second creation account in Genesis 2-3, there is nothing at all to connect sexual desire with disobedience to God and there is nothing at all to claim that matter is inherently evil. This is the story that includes the words:

> Therefore a man leaves his father and his mother and clings to his wife, and they become one flesh. And the man and his wife were both naked, and were not ashamed. (Genesis 2:24-25, NRSV).

This celebration of "clinging" and "they become one flesh" in the creation story doesn't sound much like condemnation of sexuality.

Sexuality in the Song of Solomon

The most explicit example of the celebration of sexuality in Hebrew scriptures is the erotic poem, the *Song of Solomon*, which reads like a torrid romance novel. It begins with these words:

> The Song of Songs, which is Solomon's. Let him kiss me with the kisses of his mouth! For your love is better than wine, your anointing oils are fragrant, your name is perfume poured out; therefore the maidens love you. Draw me after you, let us make haste. The king has brought me into his chambers. We will exult and rejoice in you; we will extol your love more than wine; rightly do they love you (Song of Solomon, 1:1-4).

This is probably too racy for most Christian church services but these words are part of the Bible. And it gets even racier later in this book that the Christian church calls sacred scripture.

Hebraic traditions do not involve renunciation of sexuality and they do not require celibate clergy. However, renunciation of sexuality and celibate clergy are very much a part of Christian tradition, due to the influence of pervasive Hellenistic beliefs about the inherent sinfulness of matter.

In the case of Augustine, his years among the Manicheans, beginning at the sexually eager age of seventeen, were a powerful influence on his life. His thirteen year relationship with the love of his life—the unnamed mother of his son—and his acquiescence to his mother's demand that he send her away, combine to produce a life story of love, sex, betrayal, grief, shame, and a whole lot of confusion. Augustine's life experiences are the foundation of a religious doctrine that conflates sexual desire with disobedience to God's commands and calls it sin.

Established "Anew" or Established "A New"?

This brief foray into the life of Saint Augustine raises significant questions about the connection between the salvation theology of the Christian church and its claims about the biblical foundations of the theology of original sin.

Although Saint Jerome claimed that Augustine "established anew the ancient faith," it would be more accurate to say that Augustine established "a new version" of the ancient faith. Augustine was a synthesizer of various religious and philosophical traditions.

The faith that emerged from Augustine's writings has significant differences from the ancient faiths of the Bible. Augustine's new version of the ancient faith hides your true identity from you by identifying you with a false identity as a sinner, guilty of Adam's sin at your birth. If you truly believe that this is your true identity, you will very likely remain trapped in a salvation story that fills you with guilt and shame. You will be stuck in the salvation trap.

Part Two

Your Name

and

Your Identity

Chapter 4
What Defines Your Identity?

From antiquity, people have recognized the connection between naming and power.

Casey Miller and Kate Swift

What Is Your Name?

Have you ever considered what it means that you have your own name? Not a label, but a name that is uniquely your own? Your name sets you apart from everyone else. Your name identifies you.

Not so long ago, the population of Earth reached seven billion human beings. Who are you among seven billion? You are you. Whatever your name, you are unique. Your DNA is unique. Even identical twins are never exactly identical. Even they have their own unique names.

In *I-Robot*, a movie based on stories by Isaac Asimov, one robot has a name. He is "Sonny," the creation of his "father" who designed him to be unique. This name sets him apart from all of the other robots. They are identified only by a model number. Sonny has a name. Sonny also has the capacity to dream and to value his own life. He is unique and he knows it.

Significantly, the sacrament of baptism in Christian churches is a naming ritual. You are baptized as a person who has your own unique name. Even if you have a name that is common enough that there are other people with your name, your name marks you as uniquely yourself.

However, the tendency of the Christian church, after this initial celebration of your unique identity in baptism, is to forget your name. Instead of treating you as a unique person, you are reduced to a role to serve a function and a soul to be saved.

However, you are more than a role and a soul. You are uniquely you. You have your own name.

The Unnamed You

Once, my husband Jim and I were riding in the car and passed a church. The sign out front had the name of the church and these six words:

Come to worship. Leave to minister.

I said to Jim: "There it is, in six words. The core problem of the Christian church."

These two statements are imperatives. Imperatives can be orders or invitations. No doubt, those who chose the words intended them to be an invitation to attend the church but the inherent problem of imperatives is that they are addressed to *you* without mentioning *you*.

In this case, the omission of *you* goes beyond the two imperative forms on the sign. The two invitations/commands identify the actions *you* are supposed to do:

- Come to worship

- Leave to minister

Do you notice anything missing?

What's In It for Me?

What about you? What is the benefit to *you* in attending this church?

The little I understand about sales strategies is the claim that people go through life listening to an imaginary radio station in their heads, the radio station, WIIFM. The acronym stands for, "**What's In It For Me?**"

The function of advertising is to persuade a potential customer of the benefit of buying what you are selling so that the customer will buy. This means that effective advertising answers the question, "What's in it for me?"

If you ask this WIIFM question about this sign, the question becomes: "What's the benefit for *me* to attend this church?"

If you go to worship God and then leave to serve others, how does attending church meet your needs or desires? Even this asking this question in some Christian circles can be used as evidence of your selfishness and pride, demonstrating why you really do need to worship God and serve others.

I Crossed Out

As a child growing up in a house where parents *deserved* to eat breakfast but children didn't, I went to Sunday School hungry every Sunday for years. Almost every Sunday, I heard another lesson about how we were supposed to give food to others because they were hungry based on the assumption that anyone who shows up in church needs nothing.

I heard some variation of this theme in every church I ever attended. The people *out there* deserve help. It's up to *you* to provide it. You have no needs. You must not ask for anything. You must not expect anything. You must worship the God who saved you and serve others out of gratitude for your salvation.

Some Christian preachers even reinforce this theme of self-obliteration by describing the cross as "I crossed out." You are to surrender yourself, to submit yourself, to forget yourself, as you worship the God who saved you—even though you don't deserve it—and to serve others, whose needs are more important than your own.

When I did intensive work to overcome the effects of growing up in a family terrorized by a raging alcoholic, I learned that one of the defining characteristics of alcoholic families is that children learn that they must be needless and wantless. An alcoholic family is a perfect training ground for the type of Christian theology that treats any desire or want on your part as selfishness and proof of your nature as a sinner.

Unique Stories

In my own life, the single biggest wound inflicted on me by the Christian church, in all of its forms, was that I mattered only as a role, not as a person.

This is one of the reasons why I am much more interested in stories than I am in theologies. Theologies ignore the particularities of your life, to fit you into defined roles. In contrast, life stories are unique at the same time they are universal. Stories are what set us apart and stories are what bind us.

There is no one-size-fits-all story, because not one of us is interchangeable. It's not like going to the store and buying a package of identical light bulbs. They are interchangeable. But you are unique. You are you. No one who ever lived before was just like you and no one who ever lives will be just like you. This is why you have your own life story, a story made up of thousands of stories. Your stories matter, because you matter.

A Teenager "Going through a Phase"

The first time I ever asked for help from anyone in the church occurred just before I started my second year at the University of Massachusetts. I had stayed on campus all summer, working in the Zoology Department library, and taking a chemistry class so I could stay in a dorm. The real reason I stayed on campus was to avoid going "home" for the summer.

It was actually a strange kind of reversal. Every summer, hordes of college students headed to Cape Cod, hoping to get summer jobs. Meanwhile, as a native of Cape Cod, with a lucrative job already lined up at a popular waterfront seafood restaurant, I chose to stay away and work in a campus library for minimal income.

My roommate that summer was an ardent Christian, who did her best to convince me that I had to "forgive my parents and make everything right." And so I succumbed to her nagging, and decided to go my small hometown to ask the minister of my home church to help me talk with my parents. I really did want to change the situation with my parents and had no idea how I could do that without help.

A Visit to Mr. Edwards

So I called and made an appointment with the man I will call Mr. Edwards. The name evokes one of the most notorious New England Congregational church ministers in church history, a man famous for terrorizing his parishioners with hellfire and damnation sermons.

Mr. Edwards was the third white-haired minister who served as the minister of the local Congregational church during my childhood. He was the latest in a line of ministers in their last parish before retiring. He came to the church when I was in high school. By that time, I had stopped going to church on Sunday morning, about the time my mother started to go to church. I am certain that he had never met my father. In other words, he had no firsthand knowledge of our family. Although I had met him, I didn't know him and he didn't know me, except by reputation. It was a small town with a small high school. I received a number of awards and honors in that small place during high school.

So, I rode on a bus from Amherst to Springfield, and then on another bus from Springfield to Boston, and finally on a third bus from Boston to Hyannis. The trip took all day and the round-trip bus tickets took almost every dollar I had, leaving me with no money for food on the trip.

Breaking the Rule

I was filled with dread and hope at the same time. I was going to my hometown, intending to do what I had never done before. I was going to break the single, overriding rule of my childhood: "Never tell anyone what goes on at home." I had already broken that rule when I started talking with a counselor at the university during the second semester of my freshman year. But this time, I was going to break the rule in my hometown. My deepest hope was that Mr. Edwards would help me create a new relationship with my parents.

When I got to the parsonage, Mr. Edwards greeted me warmly, invited me into his study, and invited me to sit down. The study was so dark that I felt that I was entering a cave. Before I could say a word, he said, with the kind of exaggerated friendliness of a used car salesman: "I know why you are here. You met a nice boy at college and you want to get married."

I was speechless. It took a moment for me to respond and say: "No, I want to talk about my relationship with my parents."

Although I don't remember much that either of us said in that dark study, I do remember some phrases that remained burned in my memory as if he had branded me with an iron.

One statement was: "No one like you could possibly come from a bad family. As far as I am concerned, you come from one of the finest families in the town."

By then, I was crying. The little handkerchief he had given me was beyond saturated. I was so upset that I could barely speak. But even then, I managed to say out loud what I came to ask. I asked him to help me talk with my parents.

Instead of agreeing to my request, he branded me with these words: "All teenagers go through a phase when they don't get along with their parents. You are just going through a phase. You wait and see, in a year you will come back and tell me that I am right."

By this point, I was sobbing uncontrollably, but I managed to ask one more time: "Will you help me talk with my parents?"

At that, he reached over, patted me on my left knee and said: "Let's keep this our little secret, just between you and me."

Shoved Out

Then he suddenly stood up, grabbed my arms, pulled me to my feet, pushed me out of his cave-like study, and out of the front door onto the porch. Then he shut the door behind me.

I was left standing on the front porch of the parsonage, crying, shaking, completely stunned.

As upset as I was, I realized that I had another problem. I wanted to get out of there without being seen. There was no good way to do that.

I was in my hometown, in the center of a small village made up of ten or twelve businesses in small buildings. The shoe store. The drugstore. The post office. The corner grocery market. The five and ten. The gas station. They were all postage stamp size buildings in a tiny town where "everyone knew everyone" and no one saw anything.

I had walked by those buildings hundreds of times during my childhood. I did not want to walk down that street on that day where I might encounter people I knew. I had only two other options. I could cross the street, walk past the white steepled church that looked like every other white steepled church in "historic and picturesque" New England. That route was longer, and would take me past too many houses. The best option was to go around the corner and walk down the residential street that ran parallel to Main Street. Although I would pass several houses, I was less likely to encounter anyone I knew. That route would take me to a large field, where I could go into the woods and hide out while I recovered my composure.

A "Little Secret" Betrayed

I spent that night in my parents' house, a long night filled with memories of the horrors and pains of that place. The next day, I spent another whole day on buses from Hyannis to Boston, from Boston to Springfield, and from Springfield to Amherst. My only hope after that disastrous meeting was that Mr. Edwards would in fact let my visit be "our little secret."

The fall semester started a few days later, on my nineteenth birthday. I began my sophomore year. About a week into the semester, I got an irate letter from my mother, which began with these words: "How dare you talk to Mr. Edwards about us."

So much for "little secrets" about a conversion between a clergyman and member of his congregation. I felt betrayed and violated. I wrote a short letter to Mr. Edwards asking him to take my name off the membership list of the church. I wrote nothing more. I could think of nothing else to write to someone who had proven himself so unworthy of trust.

Within a few days, I received a letter from Mr. Edwards. He wrote that he had sadly taken my name off the membership list and was sorry to hear that I was losing my faith. Clearly, Mr. Edwards was a man with an extraordinary ability to miss the point.

More than that, Mr. Edwards was a man who had reduced me to a role. Even though he was willing to see me as old enough to marry "a nice boy," when I spoke about my parents, I was nothing more than a teenager going through a phase. He had no interest in finding out the real circumstances of my life and he had no sense of pastoral obligation to keep the "little secrets" of a teenager.

The Beginning of Freedom

Here is the beginning point of freedom to be your true self. The deepest freedom you can experience in life can come only when you are free to know who you truly are. To do this, you need to recognize why so much of what you believe to be true about yourself is actually false.

My goal in *Your True Self Identity* is to create a mirror-image process of what Lakhani did for people in witness protection programs. They needed false identities to live. My claim is that Christian salvation theology hides your true identity from you behind false stories about the Bible.

My purpose is help you discover your true identity, the true identity that has been hidden from you behind layers of theological doctrine based on distortions of biblical stories. The purpose is set your true self free from the shame imposed upon you by salvation theology so that you have the freedom to claim your true identity.

Chapter 5
Your Identity as a Sinner

Whatever crushes individuality is despotism, by whatever name it may be called and whether it professes to be enforcing the will of God or the injunctions of men here.

John Stuart Mill

What Happened to Your Name?

One of the most poignant and heartbreaking demonstrations of the connection between the dominant Christian salvation story and the identity stories of believers is the experience of two hundred deaf boys at St. John's School for the Deaf in St. Francis, Wisconsin. The boys were molested by a Roman Catholic priest decades ago. Although the boys began reporting the abuse as children and continued telling their stories for decades, the story didn't become headline news until 2010.

For weeks, stories about the deaf boys and the predator priest filled the news. There were stories about priests and bishops and popes. Stories about molesters and enablers. Stories about who knew what and who covered up what. Stories about celibacy and homosexuality and laicization of priests. Stories about pedophiles and the role of therapy. Stories about crimes and sins.

Most of the emphasis was on Pope Benedict XVI in his role as pope and his earlier role as Archbishop Ratzinger. What did the Pope know and when did he know it?

For weeks, Pope Benedict remained silent.

A Wounded Church of Sinners

Finally, in April, the Pope made a statement: "I am the leader of a wounded church of sinners." Significantly, this answer is a statement about Pope Benedict's own identity.

The statement by Pope Benedict is a statement about labels and roles. Pope Benedict identified his role as the "leader." Everyone else is identified by the one label of "sinner." Consider what this means.

Your name—the name that identified you as a unique person in the ritual of baptism in most churches—is replaced by a label. Your primary identity becomes "sinner," a designation that obliterates you as a unique person.

Maybe because I grew up in the midst of name callers d was called just about every name under the sun, including mean distortions of my own name, I became acutely aware of the shaming effect of name-calling. Name-calling replaces your own name with a name chosen by the name-caller. The names chosen by name-callers are usually derogatory, demeaning, and diminishing.

Let's assume that Pope Benedict intended to speak the truth as he sees it, to provide both a diagnosis and a remedy for the wounds created by a predator priest and a church hierarchy that protected the priest and would not hear the cries for help from the deaf boys.

But from the perspective of the abused boys who are now grown men, these words demonstrate with stunning clarity another truth: Pope Benedict cannot help these men.

He cannot help them find what they are still seeking. He cannot help them find freedom from the abuse that seared their souls and kept them wounded, betrayed, and filled with rage and grief and shame. He cannot offer justice for the boys who were violated by a priest and a complicit hierarchy. He cannot undo their shattered faith and trust in God and their church.

The Dominant Christian Salvation Story

Pope Benedict's words encapsulate the dominant salvation story of the Christian church, across many denominations and sects. Even churches that agree on little else teach this story. Details vary over various theological issues but the core of the story is based on a simple identity claim.

According to this claim, your true identity is that you are a sinner. You can't change your identity because it is innate. You were born a sinner. You will live your entire life as a sinner. You will die a sinner. You cannot save yourself from your identity as a sinner. This is why you need the church. Only the church can give you what you cannot give yourself. It offers you the salvation story that will save you from your sin.

Here is the essence of the salvation story. Since your true identity is a sinner, you must be saved from your true nature by someone who is not a sinner. This is why you need to saved by Jesus, the "perfect Son of God." Jesus was the only sinless human being ever born and therefore, the only acceptable sacrifice to atone for your innate sin. Through his death and resurrection, Jesus became the savior of humanity. His death atones for the guilt of your sinful nature so that you can experience a redeemed life in a heavenly afterlife.

Why This Salvation Story Cannot Save the Innocent

This brief synopsis of the salvation story is oversimplified and leaves much room for diverse theological formulations. However, this synopsis is enough to demonstrate why the statement of Pope Benedict—"I am the leader of a wounded church of sinners"—cannot set the victims of a predator priest free.

For the victims, the salvation they have been seeking for decades is not the promise of a better life in a heavenly future, but justice and freedom from shame in *this* life.

Longing for salvation begins with the hope for a better now. The longing begins with a sense of helplessness about present circumstances that are too painful, too frightening, too overwhelming to ignore and yet too powerful to overcome. But this longing for salvation is more than a sense of helplessness. The longing is nurtured by the hope that there is more to life than what now exists. Surely someone can do something to save us, to end the pain, the fear, the frustration right now. Surely someone can provide justice and healing. Surely someone can end the shame.

Salvation Then and There, Not Here and Now

Yet despite this abiding hope for a better now, the dominant Christian salvation story changes the time of salvation from the present to the future and the location from Earth to Heaven. What is the result of this change in time and location?

- Instead of freedom from pain and shame in this life on Earth, believers are promised freedom in the next life in Heaven.

- Instead of providing hope for healing wounded bodies and broken hearts in this life, believers are promised wholeness in a future life without sorrow, grief, and suffering.

- Instead of providing justice for the innocent, believers are promised forgiveness of their own sins.

It's this displacement of salvation from *now to then* and *here to there* that makes salvation theology such an impotent doctrine for justice and healing. And most significantly, this displacement turns this salvation doctrine into such a potent weapon of shame against the innocent.

The Missing Piece

Instead of making priests, bishops, and popes the focus of attention, let's start over and focus on the victims by asking a different question.

How does the salvation story of Jesus as the perfect savior of sinful humanity set free two hundred deaf victims of a predator priest from the lasting effects of the harm done to them?

Anyone who truly asks this question will immediately see that the statement of Pope Benedict is flawed. The stunning omission from the statement by Pope Benedict is that the boys were *innocent.*

The words, "I am the leader of a wounded church of sinners," makes clear that the salvation story he offers depends on one foundational assumption: No one is innocent, except Jesus, the sinless savior.

When it comes to offering salvation from grief, pain, injustice, and suffering in this life, this particular salvation story has very little to offer to the deaf victims of a predator priest. Even deaf boys raped by a priest are sinners who need to be forgiven.

This is why Pope Benedict cannot provide true healing to innocent victims. He has only one remedy—forgiveness of sins. This is a theology of guilt with no acknowledgement that the real need of the victims is to be set free from shame.

The Difference between Guilt and Shame

The difference between guilt and shame is a critical aspect of Your *True Self Identity.* The essential difference is that *guilt is about what you do* and *shame is about what you are.* In other words, guilt is about actions and shame is about identity.

The identity claim, "I am the leader of a wounded church of sinners," intended to convey the core salvation story of the Christian church, has one profound effect. These words obliterate the victims.

This is the deepest wound of all. It's horrifying enough to be raped by a priest and then scared into silence because the priest claims to speak for God. It's even more horrifying to be told repeatedly that you must ask forgiveness for your sins because no one is innocent before God.

Why This Salvation Story Cannot Set the Victims Free

This is why the deaf boys who are now men cannot be set free by this dominant Christian salvation story. This salvation story saves sinners from their sinful natures. How can such a story save innocent victims from crimes against them? How can it set innocent victims free from their shame?

It all comes back to the question of identity. Who are you? The dominant salvation story of the Christian church rests on this one claim: Your true identity is that you are a sinner and you must be saved from your sinful self. This doctrine itself is a weapon of shame.

Subliminal Persuasion

Before you take this as some sort of blanket indictment of the Christian church, including Pope Benedict, please understand my real point. The power of this salvation story to create false identities for Christian believers has been so much a part of Western culture for at least sixteen hundred years that it has gone far beyond any intentional manipulation to become *subliminal persuasion* on a massive scale.

Dave Lakhani defines subliminal persuasion this way:

> The essence of subliminal persuasion is the message: the message your audience, hears, receives, and experiences as being true (Lakhani 2).

In other words, you don't have to be persuaded to believe what you already believe to be true.

By now, the message that Jesus died on the cross to save sinners from their sins to ensure life in Heaven after death is so deeply embedded in common belief that it is rarely challenged, either by believers or non-believers. Even people who do not believe that God exists, do not believe that Jesus existed, and do not believe that the Bible is divinely inspired, do believe that the Bible teaches that Jesus died on the cross to save sinful humanity from our sins.

This is exactly the point I intend to challenge. My claim is that the salvation stories of the Christian New Testament gospel stories bear little resemblance to the dominant Christian salvation story.

Part Three

The Bible

and

Your Identity

Chapter 6
Gatekeepers of Your Identity

When distant and unfamiliar and
complex things are communicated to
great masses of people, the truth
suffers a considerable and often a
radical distortion. The complex is made
over into the simple, the hypothetical
into the dogmatic, and the relative into
an absolute.

Walter Lippmann

This Is the New Testament

Have you ever pondered the fact that every English-language Bible is a translation? One of my enduring memories from theological seminary is the time when one of my New Testament professors held up a Greek New Testament, waved it in the air, and said: "This is the New Testament. Everything else is a translation."

Whatever your theological beliefs about the truth of the Bible, if you are reading the Bible in English, you are reading a translation. A translation of the Bible is not as simple as the translation of a contemporary novel that was written in another contemporary language and translated into English. The printed Bible you hold in your hand is the product of centuries of human actions to write, preserve, transmit, and translate ancient documents.

This means that Bible translators are *gatekeepers* of information. Throughout history, gatekeepers controlled access to cities by controlling the city gates. In the late twentieth century, "gatekeepers" took on a metaphorical meaning related to mass media. Media gatekeepers decide what messages will be distributed and what messages will be withheld.

This *gatekeepers* description is especially relevant for Bible translators. Their mass medium is the most widely printed book in the world. In recent years, their mass medium can also include audio versions of the most widely printed book in the world.

Unlike bestsellers that come and go, some translations of the Bible endure. Consider the lasting effects of the King James Version (KJV), which was first published in 1611. For many of the last four hundred years, the KJV has been considered "The" authoritative English Bible, often by people who seem to have little understanding that they are reading a translation, not a book that was dictated by God in King James English.

Who Are the Translators?

Unlike most books, whose authors are named on the front cover, most translations are the work of committees. (You can probably find out the names of the translators by contacting the publisher. You usually won't find them listed in the books themselves.) This means that the decisions of Bible translators—small armies of nameless and faceless scholars toiling behind the scenes—imbue the words on the page with the credibility and authority of Holy Scripture. For those who regard the Bible as "the inerrant and infallible Word of God," the words of translators become words of God.

Shortly before I began my doctoral study, I had a conversation with a woman I had just met. In the course of the conversation, I told her that we had just moved to California so that I could go to school in Berkeley. She expressed great interest in the program and asked more about what I was going to study. I told her that I had to fulfill language requirements for six languages, including the four ancient languages of Biblical Greek and Hebrew, as well as Latin and Aramaic, and modern German and French, at different levels of reading proficiency. She asked, "Why bother learning the languages? Why don't you use translations?" I said to her, "Biblical scholars are the ones who do the translating."

At that point, even I didn't realize the full significance of my own statement. In fact, ability to read the Bible in its original languages is the essential skill and defining distinctive of biblical scholars. The ability to begin with the original languages separates biblical scholars from scholars in most other fields of study related to religion, including theologians, who may or may not be able to read the original languages.

If you can't read the original languages, you are dependent on translators. Translators—no matter how dedicated or skilled—are finite human beings. All human beings are limited by our experiences, environments, and perceptions, and limited by our own knowledge, beliefs, and intentions. These human scholars become the gatekeepers for what you will read and what you will not read on the pages of your Bible.

Translation as the Telephone Game

The whole process of writing, preserving, transmitting, and translating ancient documents can fairly and accurately be described with another metaphor—the "telephone game."

The telephone game is the most common name in the United States for a game played around the world. The game is called by a variety names, in many languages. English names include "Chinese whispers," "grapevine," and "broken telephone."

The game begins with one person who whispers a message to another, who whispers the message to the next person. As the whispered message passes from person to person, the message is usually changed. Some players hear the message incorrectly. Some players change it deliberately. By the time the last person announces the message to the whole group, the message is usually changed significantly.

Chinese whispers—the most common name for the game in the United Kingdom—is especially appropriate because it gets to the essence of the problem of translating manuscripts written in ancient languages in the ancient world into contemporary languages:

> Today, the name "Chinese whispers" is said by some to be considered offensive or racist, although it is still commonly used in the United Kingdom and is not known to cause offence to the Chinese themselves. Historians trace Westerners' use of the word Chinese to denote "confusion" and "incomprehensibility" to the earliest contacts between Europeans and Chinese people in the 1600s, and attribute it to Europeans' inability to understand and appreciate China's radically different culture and worldview. Using the phrase "Chinese whispers" suggested a belief that the Chinese language itself is not understandable ("Chinese whispers," *Wikipedia*).

This is why every translation is an interpretation, based on centuries of "playing the telephone game" with ancient documents. It's impossible for any translation to be neutral. Every translation has its own agenda and its own purposes. Some purposes are stated explicitly. These are the decisions that are explained in prefaces of translations. Some purposes are implicit. These are the decisions the translators feel no need to explain. And some purposes are unintentional.

Lost in Translation

It's the unintentional purposes that are the real problem. They are the unchallenged assumptions of the translators' own era, the unchallenged assumptions of their own theological beliefs, the unchallenged assumptions of their own life experiences, without sufficient appreciation of the fact that every part of the Bible involves writings, societies, and beliefs from a long, long time ago.

Even now, we refer to meanings that become "lost in translation" from one language to another.

Even communication between native English-speakers from different English-speaking countries can get a bit "lost in translation."

Even in the same country, various regions have their own unique expressions, which can sometimes lead to meanings getting lost in translation.

For example, on Cape Cod, when I grew up, soft drinks were called "tonic." In the restaurant where I started working when I was fourteen, it took me a day or two to realize what the tourist customers wanted when they asked for "soda." I also realized that I had to interpret the word "tonic" on the menu for some incredulous customers who couldn't believe their ears at the quaint expressions of the local yokels. After all, "everyone knows" that the stuff is "soda."

If you have done any traveling at all in your life, you can surely come up with your own experiences of amusing, confusing, and odd encounters with people who don't speak quite the same language you speak, even if the words are in English. For one example among many, I remember the time when a group of us ate dinner in a hotel restaurant in St. Petersburg, Russia. The waitress asked if we wanted water "with or without gas." It took a moment or two for someone to realize that she was asking if we wanted what

Americans are most likely to call "sparkling" or "carbonated" water.

In addition, each generation has its own jargon and its own expressions. Words become dated. Meanings of words change. Some words fall out of use. New words are created. This is why English is a constantly evolving language. This is also why people feel the need to have new Bible translations as old translations become more and more dated.

Yet, these differences in our own times and places are minor compared to the difficulties involved in working with long dead languages from ancient cultures. This is the challenge for Bible translators as they attempt to understand what ancient writers really intended in ancient languages, in societies that were dramatically different from our own.

My intention in all of this is to call attention to the often unexamined power of translators to be the gatekeepers of what you read in any Bible translation as preparation for looking carefully at a specific verse in the Gospel of Matthew.

Chapter 7
The Effect of Sin Juice
On Your Identity

We are taught as children to respect
authority figures. When an authority
figure hurts us and we minimize their
responsibility or blame the victim, that's
the individual and society as a whole
becoming confused.

Deborah Gust

The Gospel of Matthew and the Abuse of Children

Earlier, I quoted Pope Benedict's long-awaited response to
the outrage engulfing the Roman Catholic church
concerning the two hundred deaf boys molested by a priest.
The answer, "I am the leader of a wounded church of
sinners," explains why these men are still seeking the
freedom that eludes them and still demanding to be heard
by a deaf church.

Pope Benedict's answer emerges from the pervasive sin
theology of the Christian church and its dominant salvation
story—Jesus saves sinners from their sinful selves. This
answer obliterates the deaf boys, who as grown men, are
still seeking justice and still seeking salvation from the
guilt, shame, betrayal, and horror of their experiences.

In contrast, questions that begin with, "What would
Jesus in the Gospel of Matthew say," provide dramatically
different answers about the abuse of children by religious
leaders.

Why Choose the Gospel of Matthew?

Why choose the Gospel of Matthew instead of other biblical books? If you read the Gospel of Matthew, as it is written, it is one of the most devastating condemnations of the abuse of children, and other vulnerable people, anywhere in the Bible. However, it can be difficult to see the intensity of this condemnation in contemporary English translations because the Greek of the Gospel of Matthew has been translated through the filter of the doctrine of original sin and the salvation story created by this doctrine. Let me demonstrate a glaring example in the translation of Matthew 18:6.

What Did Jesus Say about the Little Ones in Matthew 18:6?

The guiding principle of biblical scholarship is to set verses in context rather than to begin and end with verses ripped out context and made to stand alone.

The larger contexts of any particular story are both the *whole story* of the story itself and the *Whole Story* in which the story is set.

In *Stealing Fire from the Gods*, James Bonnet defines the Whole Story as "The larger background or frame story that…creates the context for the story focus" (Bonnet 261).

Instead of beginning with *whole story* of the Gospel of Matthew or the *Whole Story* of first century Palestine, I'll begin by focusing on one Bible verse to show you how changing one word in one verse of the Gospel of Matthew distorts "what Jesus says" into something that *Jesus did not say*.

Later, we'll put this one verse in its larger contexts, but for now, let's look at Matthew 18:6 in the *Common English Bible* (CEB).

I cite this translation because it's the newest complete translation of the Bible in English. The CEB *New*

Testament was first published in 2010. The entire CEB *Bible* was published in 2011, the 400th anniversary of the publication of the King James Bible. Its motto in the frontispiece is this: "A fresh translation to touch the heart and soul."

The Common English Bible Translation of Matthew 18:6

Under the heading "falling into sin" (without capitalization) the CEB provides this translation:

> falling into sin
>
> As for whoever causes these little ones who believe in me to trip and fall into sin, it would be better for them to have a huge stone hung around their necks and be drowned in the bottom of the lake (Matthew 18:6, CEB).

What do you think about this statement as an answer to the question: "What does Jesus say in the Gospel of Matthew about the abuse of children by religious leaders?"

"The little ones who believe in me" seems to fit the category of religious belief. Jesus' judgment is extremely strong. It would be better for "them" to be drowned with a huge stone around their necks. But what exactly what did "they" do?

Ah, here it is: "Whoever causes the little ones to trip and fall into sin..."

Really? How is this any better than saying, "I am the leader of a wounded church of sinners"? Both the statement by Pope Benedict and the CEB translation of Matthew 18:6 turn children and "little ones" into sinners because of the actions of religious leaders against them.

I don't have adequate words to express the depth of my dismay as a biblical scholar at the CEB translation. A translation that claims to offer "a fresh translation to touch the heart and soul" demonstrates the insidious problem of the salvation trap.

This translation distorts what Jesus in the Gospel of Matthew actually says clearly in Greek and turns it into an assertion of sin theology.

The Bible Soaked in Sin Juice

Both Pope Benedict's words and this translation demonstrate the same overwhelming influence of sin doctrine in Christian history. It's as if the Bible got tossed into a vat of *sin juice* and transformed, the way tossing crunchy, sweet cucumbers into a brine solution turns them into sour pickles.

The result is a translation that is so infused with sin doctrine that what Jesus says in Matthew is turned into a reinforcement of sin theology. It also means that what Jesus actually does say about religious abuse of little ones is turned into another weapon against the vulnerable, to keep them shamed, guilty, and powerless.

Good Intentions

In addition to the mistranslation itself, what makes this 2010 translation so dismaying is because it's all done with such good intentions.

Before I show you how the CEB translation distorts the Greek of Matthew 18:6, I want to make clear that I don't think the translators of the CEB set out to distort anything. Actually, I think they meant to do exactly the opposite. They really did set out to create a new translation that makes the Bible accessible and understandable for believers in the twenty-first century.

If you read the Preface, you will read an ardent statement of good intentions, including this statement:

The CEB translators balance rigorous accuracy in the rendition of ancient texts with an equally passionate commitment to clarity of expression in the target language" *(CEB viii).*

They refer to the "one hundred and fifteen biblical scholars from twenty-two faith traditions" who worked as translators. They explain a range of translation decisions including decisions about manuscripts, weights and measures, use of contractions to make the translations less formal, use of gender inclusive language rather than masculine language, such as the use of plural possessive pronouns with singular subjects to avoid gender bias. They explain their intention to replace archaic language with contemporary language, easily understood by contemporary English speakers in the twenty-first century.

This translation is the work of people who really do want to get it right and provide the best translation possible. I honor their good intentions and acknowledge the extraordinary amount of effort involved in such a project. I also acknowledge how extraordinarily difficult such a project can be. I am sure they meant well, which makes the result even more dismaying.

Greek and Grammar

The CEB translation of Matthew 18:6 in fact distorts the Greek, but it does so in such comfortable, familiar language that most people have no way of knowing how the translators have become gatekeepers who have blocked access to the real meaning of these words in Greek.

To understand what happened here, we have to look beyond any English translations to see what Jesus in Matthew 18:6 says in Greek and we have to look at basic grammar.

If your first inclination when you read the words "Greek" and "grammar" is to skip over this stuff, I urge you to read the next two chapters carefully.

My own personal experience is that my liberation from mistranslated Bible verses began when I started to learn Greek and Hebrew. Only then, I began to grasp little glimpses of how often English translations obscure the most essential insights behind theological filters. I began to see glimmers of new perspectives that I could never have seen by reading one hundred English translations.

I also can trace my most significant insights and Aha! moments to tiny, nitpicking details that opened up new perspectives I would never have seen without them.

It's something like that old proverb, "For Want of a Nail":

> For want of a nail the shoe was lost.
>
> For want of a shoe the horse was lost.
>
> For want of a horse the rider was lost.
>
> For want of a rider the message was lost.
>
> For want of a message the battle was lost.
>
> For want of a battle the kingdom was lost.
>
> And all for the want of a horseshoe nail.

Beyond my own personal experiences, I urge you to read this material carefully, even if seems like boring grammatical nitpicking to you. The missing horseshoe nail is hidden in these details. This is my promise to you: This little bit of Greek and grammar holds an essential insight that can make the difference between being stuck in the salvation trap and being free.

I'll do my best to make it clear. If it is unclear to you at first, all I ask of you is that you do your best to understand what I have laid out before you. You will then be in a much better position to discover the unexamined assumptions and claims that can keep you stuck in the salvation trap. More importantly, these details can show you how to set yourself free to claim your true self identity.

Chapter 8
Identity Questions in Matthew 18:6

> Nothing has such power to broaden the
> mind as the ability to investigate
> systematically and truly all that comes
> under thy observation in life.
>
> Marcus Aurelius

Who Does What?

Matthew 18:6 identifies an action that justifies capital punishment. According to Jesus, if anyone does this action, that person deserves death by drowning. But what is this action, who does it, and who is the victim?

It's time to investigate Matthew 18:6 with the eagle-eyed precision of a detective. The detective is a staple of literature, movies, and television, including such classic notables as Sherlock Homes, Miss Marple, Detective Colombo, Sergeant Friday, Hercule Poirot, Jim Rockford, Kojak, and Jessica Fletcher. This list barely scratches the surface of fictional detectives. What all of these detectives have in common is that they look for clues—the tiny, insignificant details that no one else notices—in a determined effort to find out "whodunit."

So, in honor of all detectives—whether fictional or actual—let's grab a magnifying glass and do some serious sleuthing.

We'll begin with the grammar here and continue with the Greek in the next chapter, by beginning with a simple sentence in English.

A Simple Sentence

The essential item in any sentence is the *verb*. A verb describes an action or state of being. Without a verb, you don't have a sentence.

A simple sentence is a *clause*. A clause has a subject and a predicate. The predicate includes the verb.

Consider this sentence: "Fred kicks the cat."

- "Fred" is the **subject** of the sentence because Fred does the action of the verb.

- "Kicks" is the **verb**, which identifies the action Fred does.

- "The cat" is the **direct object** of Fred's kick.

Poor cat. Fred is the one who does the kicking. The cat is the object of the kick. What does the cat do? We don't know. The cat is the direct object of the kick. The sentence doesn't tell us what the cat does because the cat has no verb of its own.

Fred could kick the lamp post, the football, the tire, the habit, or the bucket. In all of these cases, the lamp post, the football, the tire, the habit, or the bucket, don't do anything. Each is the object that receives Fred's kick.

Actions and Consequences

Now let's complicate the sentence by adding a second clause to create a *conditional sentence*.

A simple sentence has one clause. A conditional sentence has two clauses. An *independent clause* can stand alone as a complete sentence. A *dependent clause* cannot stand alone even though it has a subject actively doing the action of the verb.

In a conditional sentence, the first clause—the dependent clause—identifies the condition. The second clause—the *consequence clause*—identifies the result of the subject's action. Conditional sentences have the sense of "if this happens, then that will happen," even if they don't use these specific words.

"Fred kicks the cat" is an independent clause. It can stand alone as a complete sentence.

However, "If Fred kicks the cat..." is not a complete sentence. It is a conditional dependent clause and needs another clause in the sentence to identify the consequence of the action.

Here are few possible conditional sentences with consequence clauses about Fred and his action of kicking the cat:

- If Fred kicks the cat, then Fred will get hurt.

- If Fred kicks the cat, the cat will get hurt.

- If Fred kicks the cat one more time, he will lose his Boy Scout good citizenship badge.

- Whenever Fred kicks the cat, the cat's owner calls the police.

- But if Fred kicks the cat, he will feel ashamed of himself.

- Anytime Fred kicks the cat, the cat hides under the porch.

It's even possible that more than one of these consequences will happen if Fred kicks the cat.

"If Fred kicks the cat, then Fred will get hurt, the cat will hide under the porch, Fred will lose his Boy Scout good citizenship badge, the cat's owner will call the police, and Fred will be ashamed of himself."

Whatever the specific result in Fred's case, Fred's kick will result in some consequence, either to himself, or to the cat, or to both of them.

Matthew 18:6

Why is this kind of grammatical nitpicking important for Matthew 18:6? It's important because Matthew 18:6 is a sentence with two clauses. The first clause is the dependent conditional clause. The second clause is the result.

In Matthew 18:6, the second clause is a *zero conditional* conveying a universal statement: Anyone who does this deserves this result.

The entire sense of the sentence depends on what the subject of the sentence does and the consequences of this action. Who does what? Who or what is affected by this action? What are the consequences and to whom?

In this chapter, we'll look very carefully at three different English translations of this verse. My emphasis here is on the relationship between the condition in the first clause and the consequence in the second clause, without getting too bogged down into the finer points of conditional sentences.

We'll also look at translations decisions concerning the use of masculine singular pronouns.

In the next chapter, we'll look at the translation of the verb in each of these three translations.

Matthew 18:6 in Greek and English

Although we'll come back to the Greek in the next chapter, here is Matthew 18:6 in Greek. I include the Greek here for anyone who has studied Greek.

Matthew 18:6 in Greek.

Ὃς δ᾽ ἂν σκανδαλίσῃ ἕνα τῶν μικρῶν τούτων τῶν πιστευόντων εἰς ἐμέ, συμφέρει αὐτῷ ἵνα κρεμασθῇ μύλος ὀνικὸς περὶ τὸν τράχηλον αὐτοῦ καὶ καταποντισθῇ ἐν τῷ πελάγει τῆς θαλάσσης (Matthew 18:6, *The Greek New Testament*, UBS).

If this really is "all Greek to you," it will become clearer when you see the Greek words rewritten in the Latin alphabet we use for English words:

> hos d' àn skandalízē héna tōn mikrōn toútōn tōn pisteuóntōn eis emé sumphérei aútō hína kremasthē múlos onikòs perì   tòn tráchēlon aùtoû kaì katapontisthē èn tô pelágei tês thalássēs (Matthew 18:6, *The Greek New Testament,* UBS).

Three Translations

Here are three translations of Matthew 18:6.

Matthew 18:6 in the King James Version (KJV)

> But whoso shall offend one of these little ones which believe in me, it were better for him that a millstone were hanged about his neck, and [that] he were drowned in the depth of the sea (Matthew 18:6, KJV, 1611).

Matthew 18:6 in the New Revised Standard Version (NRSV)

> If any of you put a stumbling block before one of these little ones who believe in me, it would be better for you if a great millstone were fastened around your neck and you were drowned in the depth of the sea (Matthew 18:6, NRSV, 1991).

Matthew 18:6 in the Common English Bible (CEB)

As for whoever causes these little ones who believe in me to trip and fall into sin, it would be better for them to have a huge stone hung around their necks and be drowned in the bottom of the lake (Matthew 18:6, CEB, 2010).

Two Clauses

Matthew 18:6 in Greek has two clauses.

The Conditional Clause

The conditional clause is:

hos d' àn skandalízē héna tōn mikrōn toútōn tōn pisteuóntōn eis emé

- The conditional particle is *d' àn*, which indicates that this is a conditional clause.

- The subject is *hos,* (masculine, singular, relative pronoun), which identifies the one who does the action of the verb.

- The verb is *skandalízē*, (third-person, singular, active, subjunctive), which identifies the action the subject does.

- The direct object is *héna*, (masculine singular pronominal adjective), which identifies the one affected by the subject's action.

- *héna* is modified by two phrases, **tōn mikrōn toútōn** and **tōn pisteuóntōn eis emé**).

The Consequence Clause

The consequence clause is:

> sumphérei aútō hína kremasthē múlos onikòs perì tòn tráchēlon aùtoû kaì katapontisthē èn tô pelágei tês thalássēs

The consequence clause identifies the one who receives the consequence of the action done by the subject of the conditional clause.

The grammar is a bit complicated here, but it involves an impersonal verbal construction, two third-person, passive, subjunctive verbs, and two prepositional phrases. We don't need to sort through all of that here because the significant translation issue involves the conditional clause.

The two relevant points in all of this are:

- In this particular conditional sentence, the subject who does the action in the dependent clause is the one who receives the result of the action in the consequence clause. This is the one who deserves to be drowned.

- The consequence clause does not refer to the effect on the direct object.

Expressed more simply, this particular conditional sentence follows the format of:

> If Fred kicks the cat, Fred will get hurt.

It does not follow the format of:

> If Fred kicks the cat, the cat will get hurt.

This whole sentence is about what happens to the subject of the dependent clause. It is not about what happens to the direct object of the verb in the dependent clause.

Translation Choices

Translation Choices in the *King James Version*

> But whoso shall offend one of these little ones which believe in me, it were better for him that a millstone were hanged about his neck, and [that] he were drowned in the depth of the sea (Matthew 18:6, KJV).

In the first clause of the KJV:

- The conditional particle *d' àn* is translated as "but."

- The subject *hos* is translated as "whoso."

- The verb *skandalízē* is translated as "shall offend"

- The direct object *héna* is translated as "one" [of these little ones which believe in me].

The consequence clause makes clear that the one who "shall offend one of the little ones" deserves to be punished for his actions by being drowned with a millstone around his neck. KJV uses the generic masculine singular here.

Translation Choices in the New Revised Standard Version

> If any of you put a stumbling block before one of these little ones who believe in me, it would be better for you if a great millstone were fastened around your neck and you were drowned in the depth of the sea (Matthew 18:6, NRSV).

In the first clause of the NRSV:

- The conditional particle *d' àn* is translated as "if."

- The subject *hos* is translated as "any" [of you].

- The verb *skandalízē* is translated as "put a stumbling block before."

- The direct object *héna* is translated as "one" [of these little ones who believe in me].

In the second clause, the consequence for "any of you" if *you* do this action, is that it would be better for *you* to be drowned in the sea with a millstone around *your* neck. NRSV uses forms of the second-person "you" to translate the masculine singular pronouns.

Translation Choices in the Common English Bible

> As for whoever causes these little ones who believe in me to trip and fall into sin, it would be better for them to have a huge stone hung around their necks and be drowned in the bottom of the lake (Matthew 18:6, CEB).

In the first clause of the CEB:

- The conditional particle *d' àn* is translated as "as for."

- The subject is *hos* is translated as "whoever."

- The verb *skandalízē* is translated as "causes little ones to trip and fall into sin."

- The direct object *héna* is translated as "these" [little ones who believe in me].

In the second clause, the consequence for "them" is to be drowned in the lake with a huge stone around their necks.

The CEB has substituted third-person plural pronouns for the third-person masculine singular pronouns in the consequence clause. A significant question for this translation is the identity of the "them" who is to be drowned. Is it the singular subject of the sentence, "whoever," or the plural direct object, "these little ones who believe in me"?

In Greek, and in both the KJV and the NRSV, the sentence structure is clear. The one who does the action of the verb is the one who is to receive the consequences of the action. However, in its laudable effort to use gender inclusive language, the CEB has managed to confuse the issue.

Who Does What?

Now we get to the real grammatical heart of the matter. In a conditional clause, the subject of the sentence does the action of the active verb.

In Matthew 18:6, the Greek verb of the conditional clause is *skandalízē.* If the word looks familiar, it's because the English words *scandal* and *scandalize* are derived from Greek.

You probably have a clear idea of what these words mean in English. The real question is what the Greek root *skandal* means in the Gospel of Matthew. The fact that I have raised the question is a clue that that the most significant translation issue in this verse is the meaning of *skandalízē.* In the next chapter, we'll get to the meaning of the verb of itself. For now, we can use the English verb *scandalizes.*

The most straightforward translation of the dependent clause is:

> "But whoever *scandalizes* one of these little ones
> who believe in me..."

All of this minute detail leads up to this essential point. In a dependent conditional clause, the subject of the sentence is the one who does the action of the verb. The direct object is the one affected by the action.

In Matthew 18:6a, the subject "scandalizes one of these little ones." This whole sentence is about the consequences to one who scandalizes. The Greek says absolutely nothing about what "one of these little ones" does as a result of the actions of the subject of the sentence.

In the next chapter, you will see why all of this nitpicking matters for your life and why it can set you free from the salvation trap.

Chapter 9
How One Word
Can Change Your Identity

All our knowledge has its origins in our
perceptions.

Leonardo da Vinci

Why Do You Care What Jesus Says?

"What would Jesus say?" is a significant question for
Christians who look to the Bible for answers to life's
questions.

But this question raises so many theological and
historical questions about Jesus and the Bible that we can
get distracted from the most important question of all. Why
do you care "what Jesus says" about anything?

Really. Why do you read the Bible? Why does anything
in the Bible matter to you? Isn't it to find out what all of
these stories mean for your life?

If you don't care about "what the Bible says," nothing in
the Bible is going to have much effect on your own identity
stories. The Bible can be interesting to you—possibly
fascinating or repulsive—but reading it isn't going to affect
your belief about your true identity very much.

What the Bible Says about You

However, if you believe that these stories matter to your
life, you have invested these stories with enormous power
to tell you what to do and what to believe, not just about

95

God or Jesus or money or sex or any other topic you can imagine. Your belief that the stories matter to your life invests these stories with the authority to tell you who you are.

This is why the most persuasive effect of Bible stories is not really about theological questions or historical questions. The life changing power of the Bible is not what you think "the Bible says" about Jesus or what "Jesus said" about some topic. The real power to change your life is the result of what you believe the Bible is saying about *you*.

This is when the power of subliminal persuasion happens. While you are reading stories about Jesus, you are also creating your own story about your own identity. It's a subliminal process because you are not really aware of what is happening. You read a Bible story about "what Jesus said" to the people in the story. But while you are reading this story, something else is happening. You are reading a story about yourself. You are finding out who you are.

The Best Lie Is 90% True

Let's go back to a significant detail in Dave Lakhani's brief reference to the process of creating false identities for people in witness protection programs. He claims that "the best lie is 90% true."

His deliberately provocative language emphasizes his point. He didn't have to change every detail in someone's identity story to create a false identity. He only had to make a small change. The unstated implication behind this claim is that the change has to be significant. Changing minor details of a story is not enough. You have to find the right 10% to create a new story—a new identity—which effectively hides your true identity.

Before we dismiss all of this by assuming that a process to create false identities is relevant only to undercover narcotics officers involved in witness protection programs, this little gem of an idea reveals an essential insight that is relevant to all of us. Small changes can turn the meaning of stories upside down. This principle applies to Bible stories and statements about "what Jesus says" as much as it does to the identity stories of people in witness protection programs.

In other words, a small change in a Bible story can create a false identity story for you. Or, a small change in a Bible story can reveal your true identity, the one that lies hidden behind a false identity.

Scandalizing the Little Ones

In the last chapter, we looked at the grammar of Matthew 18:6, without translating the verb. Now it is time to look at the meaning of *skandalízē*.

The word, *scandalize*, is particularly relevant here. One of the most notable phrases, which occurs again and again in media reports about the Roman Catholic church's reaction to charges of priestly sexual abuse of children, has been the desire to "save the church from scandal."

We all have a clear sense of what *scandal* and *scandalize* mean in English. Scandal is about some conduct that causes disgrace. Merriam Webster includes two definitions with religious connotations. The first is "discredit brought upon religion by unseemly conduct in a religious person." The second is "conduct that causes or encourages a lapse of faith or of religious obedience in another."

Latin Stumbling Blocks and Greek Traps

These specifically religious definitions of *scandal* are rooted in medieval church Latin, based on the meaning of *scandalum*. A *scandalum* is defined as a *stumbling block*, a *temptation*, an *inducement to sin*, or a *cause of offense*.

This church Latin influence is manifestly evident in translations of Matthew 18 where you will see the language of "stumbling blocks," "offenses," and "sins."

But before medieval church Latin existed, ancient Greek had a more basic definition of the root *skandal*.

The basic noun form is *skándalon*. A *skándalon* was a trap with a springing device set to snare an animal, or bird, or even a human enemy.

The basic verb form is *skandalízō*, which means *to trap*. A noun or verb form with the root *skandal* occurs five times in Matthew 18:6-7. It occurs three times as a noun and two times as a verb.

The simplest way to translate these Greek words is to retain the root meaning of *skandal* in Greek and use the English word trap. In English, trap can be either a noun or a verb.

In both ancient Greek and contemporary English, trap can also be used as a metaphor. You can get caught in an actual trapping device or you can feel trapped in a dead-end job. The idea behind the metaphorical uses of trap in both Greek and English is about being stuck in some situation you can't escape.

How to Create a Lie That Is 90% True

All it takes is one small change to create a lie that is 90% true. In Matthew 18:6, the change occurs with the translation of *skandalízē*.

This small translation change, not just in the NRSV and CEB translations, but in almost all English translations, replaces the root meaning of the Greek *skándalon* as *trap*, and translates according to the medieval church Latin word *scandalum* as a *stumbling block* that causes little ones to sin.

The most notable exception is the King James translation, which used *offend*. The KJV translation actually comes closer than the stumbling block language of more recent translations to conveying the meaning here. For the King James translators, the word *offend* was not about hurting someone's feelings, but taking action against that person, in the same way that armies take offensive action against adversaries. But even this translation does not do justice to the idea of trap.

The Influence of Sin Doctrine

This word choice in the translation of *skandalízē* is clear evidence of the influence of church doctrine on translations.

What is most dismaying is that biblical scholars who spend their careers reading and studying and teaching Greek continue to perpetuate the same old translations, to keep using church Latin sin language to translate Greek texts without taking seriously that Matthew was originally written in Greek.

The dominant consensus of biblical scholarship is that the Gospel of Matthew was written sometime late in the first century, around 80 A.D. Even scholars who disagree with this dating would universally agree that the Gospel of Matthew was written in Greek *centuries* before medieval church Latin existed as a language.

In Greek, *skandalízē* and *skándalon* referred to actual trapping devices and to actions that trap, as well as metaphors about trapping and being trapped.

But Christian translations of *skandalízē* and *skándalon* are so deeply embedded in collective Christian consciousness as metaphors for stumbling, tripping, and falling into sin that the essential idea of *trap* language gets lost when it's pickled in sin juice.

Why does this matter? It matters because it turns the "little ones" into sinners. There is nothing in the Greek of the Gospel of Matthew that describes the little ones as sinners. It is only centuries of Christian translation, based on centuries of Christian doctrine about sin, which imposes this sin language on the Greek text, and in the process, replaces the root meaning of trap with metaphorical sin language.

A Sin-Free Translation

The essential point in the grammatical analysis of Matthew 18:6 is that there is nothing irregular or difficult about the grammatical construction of the clause. The grammar is easy. The only real translation challenge here is the best translation of *skandalízē*, but even that is not difficult. The root *skandal* means trap. The most straightforward translation of the dependent conditional clause is:

> "Whoever traps one of these little ones who believe in me..."

How Sin Juice Turns Little Ones into Sinners in the CEB

Let's look again at the CEB translation:

> falling into sin
>
> As for whoever causes these little ones who believe in me to trip and fall into sin, it would be better for them to have a huge stone hung around their necks and be drowned in the bottom of the lake (Matthew 18:6, CEB).

Instead of translating this regular, active, subjunctive, third-person singular verb, *skandalízē,* as the action done by the subject of the sentence, the CEB has done some grammatical black magic.

The CEB translators managed to create a complicated verbal clause, in which the subject is the causative agent but the direct object becomes the one who takes not one, but two separate actions. CEB has even added a modifying prepositional phrase to the second action out of thin air. This really is black magic of the highest order. With one word change, the direct object now becomes the actor. Direct objects in sentences don't usually get to do so much.

But here, the CEB has turned the direct object of the verb—"one of the little ones who believe in me"—into the ones who take actions, so that "these little ones who believe in me" not only trip. They also fall into sin.

By the way, the addition of the phrase, "and fell into sin," is completely unwarranted. This is the type of editorial addition to a text that scholars call a *gloss* when they refer to comments added to handwritten manuscripts by ancient scribes.

The CEB manufactured a clause out of thin air, to make sure that the reader understands clearly that the little ones are sinners. And to make sure that the reader gets the point, they include the heading "falling into sin" about a passage in which the word "sin" is never mentioned.

This grammatical contortion of a very simple clause turns the little ones into sinners and takes the responsibility off the ones who trap the little ones.

The Subliminal Effect of Sin Juice on Translations

This black magic contortion is the effect of sin juice on translations. Somehow, even when Jesus is condemning the ones who trap the little ones, translators have a way of turning "the little ones" into sinners.

Maybe they are doing it deliberately, in which case they are manipulating both the text and the readers who trust them to get the Greek right. Or maybe, it's all a process of subliminal persuasion. They don't even recognize what they are doing and contort the meaning despite their best intentions. They are so used to sin theology, which is rooted in Augustine's doctrine of original sin, that they somehow manage to turn trapped victims into sinners without challenging the pervasive influence of sin theology on Christian Bible translations.

This is evident even when the translators truly intend to translate the Greek accurately, as I believe the CEB translators set out to do.

It's something like the well-known Hans Christian Andersen story about the emperor's new clothes. Everybody could *see* the naked emperor's new clothes because everybody *knew* that he was wearing them, until a child pointed out the obvious: The emperor is stark naked and he has been conned.

If there was ever a demonstration of Dave Lakhani's point that he could create a new identity story for someone by making a small change, the translation of Matthew 18:6 is it. All the CEB had to do was change the translation of one Greek word to turn the little ones into sinners and obscure the real target of the condemnation—the ones who trap the little ones.

This is subliminal persuasion at work. When it comes to calling people sinners, the translators don't consider questioning the sin language here, even though it means contorting the Greek and not bothering to pay attention to what the word meant in the Greek language in the era when the Gospel of Matthew was written.

The essential point in all of this is that Matthew 18:6 is not about what the little ones do. It does not say that the little ones "tripped," or "stumbled," or "fell into sin."

The conditional sentence is all about the ones who trap the innocent. The clear sense of the Greek is:

> If anyone traps one of these little ones who believe in me, it would be better for that person to be drowned in a large body of water with a big rock around the neck.

Later, we'll come back to the context of Matthew 18, in the context of the whole story of the Gospel of Matthew. Within that larger context, it will be manifestly clear why Matthew 18 is about the ones who trap little ones and why it is not about little ones who "fall into sin."

Chapter 10
Gnats, Camels, and Your Identity

Most people fail in life because they major in minor things.

Anthony Robbins

A Trip Is Not a Trap

Let's look more carefully at the idea of *trap* that got lost in the KJV, the NRSV, and the CEB, as well as every other English translation I have ever seen. The CEB says that the little ones "trip." Other translations say that the little ones "stumble." How does either word convey the idea of trap?

What is a trap? It is something deliberately set to catch someone or something

Trappers set bear traps and beaver traps. Homeowners set mouse traps to get rid of mice in the pantry and gopher traps to get rid of gophers in the lawn. Plumbers add traps to the plumbing to keep diamonds rings from going down the drain. That is the essential meaning of trap. A trap is meant to catch something so that it cannot get out.

In English, the word trap is not the same as the word trip, whether it is a noun or a verb form. (By the way, English does this. The noun and the verb are the same. Greek lets you know the difference between a noun and verb.)

Imagine that you are walking down a hallway and someone deliberately puts something in front of you and you trip and fall flat on your face.

It's true you tripped. But are you trapped? When you are lying on the floor, face down, are you trapped on the floor? Unless you are seriously hurt, you can get up and walk away after you trip. You don't walk away from a trap. If you're trapped, you're stuck and can't get out.

A trip is not a trap and a trap is not a trip. And *skandalízē* is not about what you do when someone trips you. *skandalízē* is about someone setting a trap so that someone or something is caught and can't get out.

What about whatever gets caught in the trap? The whole idea of a trap is that the unsuspecting victim is unsuspecting. Even if you trip when you fall into a trap, you don't intend to do it. You fall because you don't see it or someone forces you to fall into it.

Trapping Hidalgo

An excellent example of being trapped occurs in the movie, *Hidalgo*. It's a story about a horse race in the Sinai desert in 1891, in which famed distance rider, Frank T. Hopkins, and his mustang, Hidalgo, win a race across the Sinai desert against purebred Arabian horses. It's a brutal race, in which some riders and horses are expected to die, and some do.

Hidalgo is also a story about identity. Both Frank and Hidalgo are "mixed." Frank is the son of a white army officer and the daughter of an Indian chief, whose hero's journey forces him to claim his true identity. Frank and Hidalgo are in the race because Hidalgo is a mixed breed horse. They must race to prove that Hidalgo can defeat purebred Arabian horses in an endurance race across the desert.

At one point, Hidalgo and Frank fall into a pit. Why did they fall? As Hidalgo is galloping across the desert, the bad guys emerge out of the hills on their Arabian horses and gallop on either side of Hidalgo. They are actually herding

Hidalgo, forcing Hidalgo and Frank towards a trap. The trap is a pit covered with sand, created to do exactly what it does. Hidalgo falls into the pit and is impaled on one of the pointed stakes arranged on the bottom of the pit. This is a trap meant to kill Hidalgo and leave Frank stuck at the bottom of a pit, without a horse, in the Sinai desert, close to the end of a grueling three thousand mile race.

In those conditions, Frank could not survive without his horse. Even if Frank could manage to climb out, he couldn't carry his severely injured horse out of the pit. Both are stuck in a trap.

It's not fair to blame the horse for falling into the trap and it's definitely not accurate to refer to the trap as a stumbling block. The horse and rider were forced into a trap and were stuck there because of the actions of others.

Three Additional Translation Decisions

At the same time, this translation demonstrates the unstated implication behind Lakhani's claim that the best lie is 90% true. It's not enough to change minor details in a story to create a new identity. The change has to be significant.

The CEB also includes three translation decisions here that deserve a brief mention. The easiest way to see these decisions in this translation is to compare them with the KJV and the NRSV (emphasis added):

> But whoso shall offend one of these little ones which believe in me, it were better for him that **a millstone** were hanged about his neck, and [that] he were drowned in **the depth of the sea** (Matthew 18:6, KJV).

> If any of you put a stumbling block before one of these little ones who believe in me, it would be better for you if **a great millstone** were fastened

around your neck and you were drowned in **the depth of the sea** (Matthew 18:6, NRSV).

As for whoever causes these little ones who believe in me to trip and fall into sin, it would be better for them to have **a huge stone** hung around their necks and be drowned in **the bottom of the lake** (Matthew 18:6, CEB).

A Huge Stone or a Great Millstone?

Let's start with the differences between a "millstone" (KJV), "great millstone" (NRSV), and a "huge stone" (CEB). If you look at commentaries on the Gospel of Matthew, you will see that the Greek refers to a *donkey millstone*, the kind of large flat rock pulled by donkeys to grind grain.

This is the kind of detail that gives preachers a rich source of metaphors about the huge size of the stone and the use of the stone for grinding, to describe the severity of the punishment for the one who *scandalizes* one of the little ones. Not just any old stone will do. It has to be a stone that is so big that you need a donkey to pull it.

Both the KJV and NRSV use "millstone." The CEB chose to use "stone" rather than "millstone." This probably reflects its desire to make the translation familiar to contemporary readers, because most of us don't have much daily experience with donkeys turning millstones to grind grain.

The significant question is: Does it really matter to your identity to know the differences between a millstone, a great millstone, and a huge stone? These are minor details in the story. It might be interesting to know these details, but not identity-changing.

The Bottom of the Lake or the Depth of the Sea?

What about the difference between "the depth of the sea" and "the bottom of the lake"? This is another place where preachers and biblical scholars can dive headfirst into the depths about the range of meanings of the Greek words here. If they go in one direction, they can emphasize the depths of the "sea" as a sign of the intensity of punishment for the one being drowned. If they go in another direction, they can use "lake" to make the reference more geographically appropriate to Jesus, who spent much of his life in the vicinity of the large lake called the Sea of Galilee. Both meanings are easily mined for moralistic metaphors, suitable for sermon illustrations.

Once again, the significant question is: Does it really matter to your identity to know the difference between "the depth of the sea" and "the bottom of the lake" in this verse?

Straining Gnats and Swallowing Camels

By now, you have no doubt noticed that I have great capacity to pay attention to details. At the same time, I do my best to remember the big picture. As a biblical scholar, I know all too well how easy it is to get so involved in these types of linguistic and grammatical details that it's possible to lose the forest for the trees. These types of translations decisions often fall under the category of "straining gnats and swallowing camels."

In Chapter 23 of the Gospel of Matthew, Jesus excoriates the religious leaders for *majoring in minors*, while ignoring the essence of the law—the Torah:

> Woe to you, scribes and Pharisees, hypocrites! For you tithe mint, dill, and cummin, and have neglected the weightier matters of the law: justice and mercy and faith. It is these you ought to have practiced without neglecting the others. You blind guides! You

> strain out a gnat but swallow a camel! (Matthew
> 23:23-24, NRSV).

In this case, it's not just the CEB. The NRSV and just about every other English translation in existence frequently "strain gnats" and "swallow camels." They will strain out gnats as they quibble over "huge stone" or "great millstone" or over "depths of the sea" or "bottom of the lake," while swallowing a camel that ignores the Greek meaning of *skandalízē* and contorts the grammar, to turn the innocent little ones into sinners.

When Fixing One Problem Causes Another Problem

The third translation decision worth mentioning here demonstrates how fixing one problem creates a new problem.

"Whoever" is masculine singular. Greek used masculine pronouns generically. English has done the same throughout most of its history as a language. The KJV uses generic masculine language throughout its translation. You can see that both the NRSV and the CEB have attempted to avoid masculine language to use more inclusive language. I heartily support this effort at the same time I acknowledge that it can be a very tricky goal to accomplish.

The KJV Non-Inclusive Translation

Both Biblical Greek and the KJV used masculine gender generically. The KJV uses the masculine singular "him," "his," and "he." This is consistent with the use of masculine pronouns in the Greek:

> But whoso shall offend one of these little ones which believe in me, it were better for **him** that a millstone were hanged about **his** neck, and [that] **he** were drowned in the depth of the sea (Matthew 18:6, KJV).

The NRSV Inclusive Language Translation

The NRSV changed the third person masculine pronouns to second person pronouns "you" and "your."

> If any of **you** put a stumbling block before one of these little ones who believe in me, it would be better for **you** if a great millstone were fastened around **your** neck and **you** were drowned in the depth of the sea (Matthew 18:6, NRSV).

The benefit of this translation choice is that it makes clear that Jesus is referring to the consequences to anyone who traps one of the little ones. If "you" trap one of the little ones, "you" deserve to be drowned with a big rock around "your" neck.

The CEB Inclusive Language Translation

One trend that is currently taking hold in contemporary English is the use of plural third-person pronouns to substitute for the singular "his" or the cumbersome "his or her." The CEB chose this solution. In an effort to avoid using masculine pronouns generically, the CEB uses plural pronouns in a way that creates the potential for confusion:

> As for **whoever** causes **these little ones** who believe in me to trip and fall into sin, it would be better for **them** to have a huge stone hung around **their** necks and be drowned in the bottom of the lake (Matthew 18:6, CEB).

This translation is a rather confusing mix between singular and plurals. "Whoever" is singular and "these little ones" is plural.

On this point, the CEB actually turned the construction with a singular direct object, "one," which is modified by "of the little ones," into the plural, "these little ones." Then, the CEB uses plural language in the second clause to change the grammatically masculine singular "him" and "his" into the plural pronouns, "them" and "their," to state that it would be better for "them" to be drowned with a huge stone around "their" necks.

This leads to the potential for confusion. Who is to be drowned? The singular "whoever" or the plural "these little ones"—the ones who "trip and fall into sin"? And how many necks are involved here? Is it one stone around one neck or one stone around many necks?

The CEB effort to avoid gender-biased language has the effect of muddling the meaning here on a point that is actually very clear in the Greek and in both the KJV and the NRSV. Unless you read this translation very carefully, it can seem to say that little ones who "trip and fall into sin" deserve to be drowned in some body of water with a very heavy weight around his, her, or their neck or necks.

How to Make a Sinner

After all of this detail, the bottom-line truth is this: Jesus *never* refers to children and little ones as sinners in the Gospel of Matthew. It's only the Christian church that does that, with its translations that turn the whole story of Matthew's Gospel on its head, to turn victims of religious, political, and economic abuse into sinners who need to be saved through the very institutions that abused them.

This is the salvation trap. This is the lie that is 90% true. And it is profoundly *unbiblical*. The clear intention of the Greek of Matthew 18:6 is that Jesus condemns anyone who traps the little ones. This intention will be even clearer when we put this beginning clause into the whole story context of Matthew 18.

But the CEB translation, which is doused in an overdose of sin juice, takes the focus off the condemnation that Jesus intends for "whoever" traps one of the little ones. It turns these little ones into "sinners" because they "tripped." And to make sure that no reader misses the point, the translation goes beyond simply mistranslating a verb that means trap with the word trip, it adds a theological explanation. If someone causes you to trip, you "fall into sin."

This translation effectively takes the responsibility off the one who set the trap to define the one who trips as a sinner. In the process, it completely obscures the power of trap language in Matthew.

All it took to change the story was to change one word. This word change diverts attention from the one who set the trap to the one who fell into it, by changing trap into trip. Abracadabra! You have a freshly made sinner.

How to Turn the Innocent Into Sinners

This is a transparent example of how sin theology works. It turns an explicit condemnation of perpetrators of religious abuse into a story about how victims become sinners.

In Matthew 18:6, all it took was one word change to turn the victim of religious abuse into a sinner. This changed story creates a new identity for "little ones who believe in me." They are now identified as "sinners" and *you*, as the reader, have completely lost the real meaning of this passage.

In Matthew 18, Jesus doesn't mince words as he condemns those who trap the innocent. He says that those who trap little ones deserve to be drowned with rocks around their necks. He says absolutely nothing to claim that the little ones turn into sinners because someone trapped them.

This is the beginning of a clue about what Jesus in the Gospel of Matthew would say about the deaf boys who were raped by a priest and about the church that was more concerned with protecting itself from "scandal" about its own reputation than protecting the innocent and punishing the perpetrator. It's also a clue about what Jesus might say to biblical translators who turn trap into trip and little ones into sinners, as they strain gnats and swallow camels.

This is the effect of sin juice on Bible translations. It turns Good News into Bad News.

Part Four

Mirrors

of

Your Identity

Chapter 11
The Bible as a Mirror
Of Your Identity

Literally as well as metaphorically, the
man accustomed to inverting lenses has
undergone a revolutionary
transformation of vision.

Thomas Kuhn

Your Reflection in a Spoon

The Bible can take many forms. One form is that it can be a
mirror reflecting your own image back to you. But mirror
images can be tricky because the image you see depends on
the mirror itself.

To see what I mean, I invite you to do a little
demonstration, either right now or sometime later. I
encourage you to do it, rather than just read about it. Even
if you already understand the principle, you never know
what you'll see when you look for yourself.

What Do You See?

You will need a shiny metal spoon, the bigger the better.

Hold up the spoon and look at your reflection. What do
you see?

Turn the spoon around. Look at your reflection again.
What do you see?

When you do this demonstration, you are looking at your reflection in two mirrors. Each one distorts your image in some way.

Your image on the *inside* of the spoon—the concave side—is curved. It is upside down, reversed from right to left, and larger than the image on the back side of the spoon.

Your image on the *back* of the spoon—the convex side—is also curved. It is right side up, also reversed from right to left, and smaller than the image on the concave side of the spoon.

So which is your true image? You see the problem. A spoon has two sides. If you have a concave image on one side of the spoon, you will have a convex image on the other side. You can't have one without the other. Each one distorts your image in some way.

That's the way it is with mirrors. Any mirror distorts your image. Even a flat mirror fixed on your wall gives you *mirror images*, not identical images. Here's the conundrum. You can never see yourself without some sort of mirror because you can never get outside of your own self to look at yourself. At the same time, all mirrors lie in some way.

The Bible as a Spoon

Earlier, I asked these questions: Why do you read the Bible? Why does anything in the Bible matter to you? Isn't it to find out what all of these stories mean for your life?

On the basis of these questions, I drew this conclusion:

> The life changing power of the Bible is not what you think "the Bible says" about Jesus or what "Jesus said" about some topic. The real power to change your life is the result of what you believe the Bible is saying about you.

In other words, you use the Bible as a mirror to tell you who you are. The image you see is a reflection from a spoon.

Since every mirror lies, how do you know what kind of reflection of yourself you are seeing?

Whatever you see about your identity in the Bible is always an image from a spoon. The significant question now is: which side of the spoon are you looking at?

At this point, I ask you to allow all of this to be a metaphor. Metaphors are comparisons between unlike things on something they have in common. Metaphors are even trickier than mirrors, because all metaphors fall apart if you push them too far. If you move beyond the comparison of what is similar between two unlike things, you begin to compare what is dissimilar, and then you lose the metaphor. This metaphor of the Bible as a spoon is especially tricky when you consider the difference between true and false images in a world of true and false identities.

Upside Down

As a child, one of my favorite pastimes was to climb the sugar maple tree beside my grandfather's garage. As a lifelong tree-lover, I can tell you that I have never loved a tree more than that one. One branch was almost parallel to the ground. I used to hang upside down by my knees from that branch, swinging back and forth. Healthy kids do that kind of thing all the time.

By the time we become adults, most of us either forget to hang upside down every now and then, or we couldn't hang upside down by our knees if we wanted to. With our adult feet firmly planted on the ground, we maintain our familiar perspective as we slog on treadmills or trails or office corridors, unable to change perspective enough to see the world upside down.

But it's exactly that change of perspective, both on the identity of your true self and the world around you, which lies at the heart of the story of Jesus in the Gospel of Matthew.

My claim is that a transformative biblical image is like your image on the inside of the spoon. It turns you upside down, to show you that there is something wrong with your perception of yourself.

If you are willing to let the metaphor be a metaphor and not push it so far that it falls apart, here is my premise. The image you see on the back of the spoon is the reflection of your false identity. It looks right because that is the way you are used to seeing yourself. However, when you see your image on the inside of the spoon—the upside-down image that looks all wrong—you know that that your true image is distorted.

The important point here is not the physics of light rays on curved surfaces, but that your false image on the back of the spoon will "look right" and the one from the inside of the spoon will "look wrong."

The Bible as Strange and New

In *Biblical Authority or Biblical Tyranny*, New Testament scholar, William Countryman, offers two pieces of advice about reading the Bible:

> When we feel that we understand and agree with everything we read, we should feel suspicious of ourselves...Only as long as the Bible is challenging us are we reading it fairly.

> Those things in scripture which seem odd or irrelevant or even threatening are likely to be the things most deserving of our attention (Countryman 96).

Old Testament scholar, Walter Brueggemann, offers a similar perspective on biblical authority:

> The authority of the Bible is a perennial and urgent issue for those of us who stake our lives on its testimony. This issue, however, is bound to remain

> unsettled and therefore perpetually disputatious. It cannot be otherwise, since the biblical text is endlessly "strange and new." It always and inescapably outdistances our categories of understanding and explanation, of interpretation and control. Because the Bible is "the live word of the living God," it will not compliantly submit to the accounts we prefer to give of it. There is something intrinsically unfamiliar about the book; and when we seek to override that unfamiliarity, we are on the hazardous ground of idolatry (Brueggemann 1).

I cite these two scholars, not to align myself with their beliefs and theological claims about the authority of the Bible, but because of their insistence that any use of the Bible that treats the Bible as familiar has lost its capacity to transform.

To cite Countryman once again:

> The Bible belongs forever to the past....This means that the Bible always stands outside our present...Yet the very fact that these are documents of the past means that the appearance of sameness and predictability can never be altogether true (Countryman 72).

My own argument is that many of the stories of the Bible are no longer "strange and new" but are now tamed and domesticated. The reflections we see of ourselves are the right-side-up images reflected on the backs of spoons. These familiar images don't require you to change your perspective, because everything "looks right."

Transformative Biblical Images

In contrast, transformative biblical images are like images on the inside of spoons, retinas, and parabolas. They invert images.

A true parabola concentrates light rays on one spot. It then reflects the upside-down image outward from within the parabola, to a focal point outside of itself, which turns the inverted image right-side up again.

Your retina is a surface much like the inside of a spoon. If you could see an image as it appears on your retina, it would be upside down, because of the way that your cornea-lens system refracts light to focus an image on your retina. Your brain knows that the upside down image on your retina is inverted and interprets the image so that the image you see is right side up.

It's all wonderfully fascinating—at least I think so. The point behind this small foray into the physics of light is that the Bible is also a surface that reflects images. The question is whether the image it reflects back to you is one that comes from *within* the Bible itself or is simply a reflection from the *surface* of the Bible.

Bible Study Perceptions

Much Bible study is like looking at the back of the spoon. The image on the back of a spoon doesn't come from inside the spoon. The convex surface keeps your image upright because it scatters the light rays outward. From this perspective, the Bible becomes a way to reinforce current perceptions, to tell you what your assigned role is in the existing social order.

Christian salvation doctrine has so permeated the Christian church, and its translations soaked in sin juice have become so familiar, that the Bible has lost much of its power to transform.

Bible study with the power to reveal your true identity cannot take place by looking at your reflected image on the back of the spoon. Every part of the Bible emerged in times and places dramatically different from our own. If you were suddenly transported into its world in some sort of time warp, you would feel lost and out of place.

Authentic Bible study has to go inside the world of the Bible itself, the Bible that is "forever in the past," to see what is "odd or irrelevant or even threatening," to let it be "strange and new."

If Bible study doesn't do that, if it doesn't force you to look at yourself from a different perspective, if it doesn't show the world upside down, it has no power to transform anything. And it has no power to show you how to become free of your false identity and become your true self.

Jesus as Visionary

If you are willing to enter into the world of the Bible itself, you will see that Jesus is a radical visionary. He sets out to show his listeners that their familiar right side up image is distorted from God's intention for the world.

One of his primary methods of changing perspective was telling *parables*. If you had some sort of Christian education, you very likely think of parables as little stories designed to teach moralistic lessons. That's certainly the way I learned about the parables of Jesus in Sunday School. They were little moralistic stories about being good, obedient, and serving others.

Dictionaries typically define parables this way:

> A short allegorical story designed to illustrate or teach some truth, religious principle, or moral lesson (*DictionaryReference.com*).

> A usually short fictitious story that illustrates a moral attitude or a religious principle (Merriam-Webster.com).

Such definitions do not pay sufficient attention to the connection between a *parable* and a *parabola*.

Parabolas turn images upside down. That is exactly what the parables of Jesus do when they are not turned into moralistic allegories.

This definition by Donald Capps captures the essential function of the parables of Jesus in the New Testament Gospels:

> A parable shatters one's customary ways of looking at life, turning upside down one's usual ways of perceiving reality, and is precisely not intended to teach a moral lesson (Capps 158).

This definition involves a willingness to turn upside down your usual way of perceiving reality, to see what you have never seen before. Sometimes, this means taking a hard look at your own certainties.

This is what visionaries do. They hold up spoons and say: "Look inside the spoon. See what the world has become. It's upside down. Imagine what the world can be if we turn it right side up."

However, even if the visionaries succeed in showing people that the world is upside down, the world doesn't seem to stay right side up for long. In a speech before the Antislavery Society in 1852, abolitionist Wendell Phillips said that "eternal vigilance is the price of liberty."

There are always forces at work to domesticate the most radical visions of how to turn an upside down world right side up. Freedom is hard won and easily lost.

The Bible itself—a complex, diverse, messy collection of writings spanning centuries—demonstrates how radical ideas become tamed. Parabolic curves turn into flat surfaces, parables turn into morality tales, revolutionary movements become institutions, and liberated ones become trapped in doctrines that rob them of their freedoms.

Then it's time for another visionary to come along, hold up another spoon, and say: "The world is upside down. We need to turn it right side up again."

This is what the New Testament Gospel stories do, when they are not domesticated, and made to serve the interests of the powerful. Turning the world right side up means challenging the use of religion as a weapon of power against the vulnerable.

This is what Jesus does in the Gospel of Matthew. He is a man on a mission to offer a radical vision of how a world upside down could be turned right side up. He holds up a spoon and says, "Look at what the world has become. It's upside down and out of whack. It's a world in which up is down and right is left."

My point in all of this metaphorical language is that you cannot begin to grasp what Jesus intends in the Gospel of Matthew if you don't look inside the spoon of the Bible.

Chapter 12
Love and Identity

A desire to be observed, considered, esteemed, praised, beloved, and admired by his fellows is one of the earliest as well as the keenest dispositions discovered in the heart of man.

John Adams

Comparing Jesus to Augustine

The fundamental difference between the self-images of Augustine and Jesus is the side of the spoon he looked at.

Before we go any further, I need to make some qualifications. To start with, Augustine was a historical figure and a prolific writer. He was the one who wrote about his life experiences. In contrast, we have no first-person accounts about the life experiences of Jesus. Let's get even more explicit here. We have no historical proof that Jesus ever lived. We also have no historical proof that he didn't. All we have are stories about Jesus, all written decades after a historical Jesus would have lived.

Does this mean that Jesus never existed? The only accurate answer is that it all depends on what you believe to be true. We'll come back to this question in the next chapter.

This means that comparing the self-identity stories of Augustine and Jesus falls under the category of comparing apples to oranges, or maybe even apples to footballs. Augustine's first-person account of his beliefs, feelings, and thoughts about his life experiences are categorically different from third-person narratives written by people with no first-hand knowledge of Jesus.

When Augustine looked at his image on the back of the spoon, he saw a sinner—a small, defective being who didn't even deserve to have God answer his prayers to save him from beatings. Since he saw his image right side up, he didn't question the accuracy of the image itself.

My contention is that he didn't get that image by entering into a transformative experience of the Bible, a parabolic experience that turns the world upside down. Instead, he looked at the *back* of the spoon, on an image that didn't force him to change perspective.

In contrast, Jesus in the Gospel of Matthew saw his image *inside* the spoon. Since the spoon itself turned his image upside down, he saw that something was wrong with his familiar image of himself

The Experience of the Beloved

Having made this distinction between Augustine and Jesus, I invite you to look at one episode in the life of Jesus, as reported in Matthew's Gospel, and to spend some time pondering some questions.

These questions come under the category of a *precritical* reading of the Bible. This is when you read the Bible and ask how it applies directly to you, without considering what anything in the Bible meant in its original contexts. We'll come back to a more critical reading in the next chapters, but for now, I invite you feel what you feel. This is the first step in recognizing that the image you see of yourself on the back of the spoon is a false identity.

The episode is the baptism of Jesus at the Jordan River by John the Baptist. After he is baptized, Jesus has this significant experience:

> And when Jesus had been baptized, just as he came up from the water, suddenly the heavens were opened to him and he saw the Spirit of God descending like a dove and alighting on him. And a voice from heaven said, "This is my Son, the Beloved, with whom I am well pleased" (Matthew 3:16-17, NRSV).

First, imagine the impact on Jesus of hearing this kind of affirmation of his identity, to hear that he is God's Son, the Beloved, and to hear that God is well pleased with him.

The Experience of the Sinner

Contrast these words with what Augustine believed to be true about his identity and God's concern for him. Augustine prayed to be saved from the beatings, but God didn't save him because Augustine was a sinner. As a mirror to his identity, Augustine's essential wound resulted in the doctrine of original sin, a theology of a God who didn't care about his suffering, and a lifelong experience of shame.

Before you read more, I encourage you to stop here and read these words as a mirror reflecting your own sense of identity. Put aside all beliefs you have about whether or not God exists. Put aside all beliefs you have about whether or not Jesus existed. Put aside any thoughts that Jesus was "Beloved" and God was "well-pleased" with him because Jesus was *unique*.

Your Experience as the Beloved

Instead, allow yourself to react emotionally as if these words were about you. How would you feel if you heard a voice from Heaven that you are beloved and that God is well-pleased with you? And if you can't relate to the word God, substitute Universe or Spirit or Higher Power or Self or anything else that reflects whatever belief you have about transcendent reality that goes beyond your own conscious awareness.

Simply read the words as a personal experience. How do you feel when you read these words as if they applied to you? How would you feel if you heard yourself described as "My beloved son, with whom I am well pleased? My beloved daughter, with whom I am well pleased?"

If you are willing to engage with this exercise, it would be worth your time to write down what you feel. You can't be wrong about anything you write. If you feel it, you feel it. Do your best to stay focused on your feelings and give your critical thoughts a rest. Linger as long as you need over these words.

After you have allowed yourself to feel what you feel when you read such words, consider what the Christian church teaches you to feel about yourself.

Chapter 13
Church Teaching
and
Your Identity

The only love worthy of a name is unconditional.

John Powell

Do You Qualify to Be Loved by God?

Have you ever heard in any Christian church that you are beloved and that God is well-pleased with you? It really doesn't count to hear that God loves you despite the fact that you are a dirty, rotten sinner, and that God's Beloved Son had to die on the cross to save you.

From my observations, what the Christian church typically refers to as "God's love" tends to be wrapped up in conditions and qualifications, soaked in sin juice, doused in guilt and shame, and served to you with the reminder that you don't really deserve it, so you had better be grateful...or else.

Unconditionally Beloved

I have long believed that the deepest problem for most of us is that few of us ever experience *unconditional* love, the kind of love with no strings attached. Few of us ever hear the kind of words from anyone that Jesus hears after his baptism in the Gospel of Matthew.

131

Can you imagine what difference it would make if you felt that you were loved just as you are? Not in spite of your sins, but with no mention of sins, failings, lacks, or limitations? Just to experience that you are beloved just because you are you?

Judgments about What Is Wrong with You

We live in an age in which most of us are constantly subjected to judgments about what is wrong with us. It's not just the dominant doctrine of original sin in church that never lets you forget that your true nature is that you are a sinner who needs to be saved from your human nature.

It's a psychotherapeutic culture that identifies you by neuroses, psychoses, traumas, and a slew of other diagnoses of what is "wrong" with you.

It's Twelve-Step programs that identify you in terms of addictions—life-long conditions that can only be "managed" but not overcome.

We also live in a culture that is sometimes astonishingly cruel in its willingness to call people unkind names and call it comedy.

And if that is not enough, many of us spend lifetimes nagging ourselves to fix what's "wrong with us." We're always "too much this" or "not enough that."

Two Experiences

I have two personal experiences to tell you, which are bookends of a sort. The first occurred during my student days in theological seminary. The second occurred years later, when I was deciding whether to stay within the Christian church or leave it.

The first experience happened during my third year of theological seminary. I was an intern at a church about fifty miles from my home. I spent two weekdays and Sunday morning each week working in the church. In the early stages of my internship, all I did was to go with the minister of the church as he visited church members in the hospital, in nursing homes, and in their homes.

One Sunday, about three weeks after I began the internship, I had a small part in the Sunday worship service. That meant I sat facing the congregation for the entire service, with an unobstructed view of everyone seated in the pews in front of me.

From that vantage point, I realized that everyone I knew by name was suffering in some way. I knew their circumstances because I had met them in their homes. I saw the woman I knew could not see me because she was losing her vision to glaucoma. I saw the man who was grieving the sudden death of his wife. I saw the couple who were losing their business. Everyone I knew by name was in some sort of pain. However, there they were, in church on Sunday morning. Why? What did they want? What did they expect? More significantly, what did they get?

What Is Right with You?

I remember the flash of insight that occurred to me: "These people do not need to be told what is wrong with them. They need to know what is right with them."

I never forgot that moment and that insight. When I began to preach sermons in worship services, that insight become my guideline for every sermon I preached. I always reminded myself that no one really knows what pains and burdens other people are carrying. Most people don't really need one more diagnosis of what is wrong with them, with a list of what they "should do" or "should not do." Instead, the deepest need for most people I have ever met is that they need to know what is right with them. Not "I'm okay, you're okay" simplistic affirmations, but real affirmation of their true selves.

But this is not what most people hear in Christian churches, at least not in any of the Christian churches I have attended. In the name of the Christian gospel—"Good News"—you hear that Jesus died on the cross to save you from your innate human sinfulness. You hear that you must confess your sins and ask forgiveness. You hear that you must serve other people with little regard for yourself. You hear that God loves you, but it is the kind of conditional love that begins with the premise that you really don't deserve it.

My own personal rule for preaching sermons was that I would never use the word "should" or its cousins, "must," "have to," or "ought to" in a sermon. I never preached "feel good" sermons, full of simplistic folksy stories. I didn't tell jokes and stories cribbed from "sermon illustrations for preachers" books. Instead, I did my best to delve deeply into the biblical texts included in the lectionary readings for that Sunday and find the real good news in them, the good news that treats every human being as valuable and worthy of love.

Is This "Speaking Prophetically"?

As I write this, I remember many of the young men of the seminary when I was a student. They walked around saying, "I can't wait to get into the pulpit and speak prophetically." As far as I could tell, their idea of speaking prophetically was to find ways to blast congregations about their "disobedience to God."

Many of these same young men also took it upon themselves to "speak prophetically" to the handful of women students at the seminary—there were five of us in the first year class in a school with more than seven hundred male and three other female students. Their self-ordained mission to "speak prophetically" to us made our student days a test of endurance as they demanded to know how we could be "disobedient to God by studying for the ministry."

Their intimidation was so intense that the five of us who began the fall semester turned into three by the end of the first semester and two by the end of the second. Of the two of us who were left, the other woman spared herself much of the harassment because she told the pack of prophets-to-be that she never intended to seek ordination. She was only studying for the degree that she thought would be a better "career option" for teaching Christian education. I escaped much of the harassment because I didn't live at the school and didn't eat all of my meals in the cafeteria seven days a week.

Blasting congregations about their disobedience to God is not the kind of preaching that *speaks truth to power*, based on biblical visions of justice. It is simply bullying in the name of obedience to the authority of scripture.

Invariably, when I preached, as an intern, a member of a congregation, or as a guest preacher in other congregations, many of my listeners sat in rapt attention. After the service, I heard words of gratitude and statements about "the best sermon I have ever heard." Even then, I didn't think such comments were about my preaching skills as much as a deep sense of gratitude for hearing something good about themselves for a change.

I think that such comments emerge from a deep longing within each of us to know that we are loved for who we are and that we matter...and that the Christian church, on the whole, fails miserably at fulfilling this deep longing.

Forgiveness for the Sin of Being Human?

The second experience is also about another insight from a church service. That particular service was an Ash Wednesday service in a large urban church.

Beyond my own personal reasons for finding church more and more untenable, I had reached the point that I was feeling an ethical conflict about whether to accept a position as a seminary professor. Although I loved teaching and studied for my doctorate so that I could teach biblical studies in a theological seminary, I began to think that continuing to teach seminary students would be something like a vegan who teaches students how to be butchers or a pacifist who trains commando forces. I didn't see how I could train clergy for ministry in churches bound to the doctrine of original sin without compromising my own integrity as a teacher and biblical scholar.

The Ash Wednesday liturgy was so steeped in sin juice that it was an exercise in ritual self-condemnation. We each received a typical church bulletin—pieces of paper, folded in half—with the words of the liturgy printed on it. The liturgy included confessions, responsive readings, and prayers. Since I no longer have the bulletin, I can't cite it exactly, but I am confident that I remember the essence of the service.

The confessions consisted of a long list of sins: "We have sinned against you by what we have done and what we have left undone. We have not loved our neighbor as ourselves." The list went on and on. The gist of the long list was that we are all sinners because we do not meet all the needs of all the people all the time—in essence, we are sinners because we are not God.

I was struck by how much the confessions of sin resembled the descriptions of what Twelve-Step programs refer to as codependence. Codependence involves taking care of the needs of others while ignoring your own needs.

At the same time, this ritual had little to do with confession of guilt for real harm done to others. There was no place in the liturgy for any sort of acknowledgement of particular sins, particular offenses, and particular injuries. It was a one-size-fits-all confession about generalities.

What about the Ashes?

The liturgy moved on to language about *ashes*. There are actually two distinct symbolic meanings of ashes in the Hebrew Bible. The first meaning is that ashes are a sign of mortality. We are finite beings. We are born. We live. We die. This is the language of "ashes to ashes, dust to dust," beginning with the reference in Genesis 3:19:

> By the sweat of your face you shall eat bread until you return to the ground, for out of it you were taken; you are dust, and to dust you shall return" (Matthew 3:19, NRSV).

Ashes are a symbol of what it means to be a finite human being on planet Earth.

The Bible also contains references to ashes, in both the Hebrew Bible/Old Testament and in the New Testament, as signs of penitence and repentance for offenses and omissions.

But the liturgy combined these two symbolic meanings of ashes of repentance and mortality, so that ashes are not only a sign of repentance for real offenses, they also become a symbol of sin because we are finite, mortal beings.

The ultimate diagnosis of the liturgy, with its confessions of the sin of not meeting all the needs of all the people all the time, and the confusion of categories about the ashes, is that we are sinners because we are mortal and we must ask forgiveness for being human and not being God.

After these confessions of sin, the pastor pronounced forgiveness. The liturgy assured us that our sins had been cast away, "as far as the east is from the west," never to be remembered again.

I thought: Even this is a lie. Because the next time we go to church, we are going to have to ask for forgiveness again in the same words.

The Language of Love

After all of this confession and forgiveness for being human, the liturgy somehow shifted into the language of love, to assure us of how much God loves us, despite all of our sins. There was nothing in what came before that justified the sudden introduction of love-language.

As a matter of logic, the whole liturgy was an argument based on shifting premises. Underneath it all, the fundamental claim is that you are a sinner because you are human.

As a matter of love, the liturgy claimed that God loves you so much that God will forgive you for your sin of being human.

Shamed Into Love?

The whole service was a ritual of shame about the "sin" of being born human. I wrote on the outside of the bulletin: "You cannot shame people into love."

How can such a ritual help any of us become truly who we are? Shame is exactly what the sin language of the church does to people. It shames people for being human, and then claims that God loves you despite your sin of being both finite and mortal. This shaming ritual has very little to do with forgiveness of real guilt for harm done to others and absolutely nothing to do with healing wounds caused by the harmful actions of others.

The Difference between Guilt and Shame

Guilt and shame are not synonyms. Guilt is the result of what you do or don't do. Shame is the result of being demeaned for who or what you are. From my perspective, the confusion about the difference between guilt and shame is the massive blind spot of the Christian church. The guilt language of the Christian church often ignores the difference between the guilty and the innocent, between sins and wounds, between what you have done or not done, and who you are.

This Ash Wednesday ritual—ostensibly offered to forgive the guilt caused by your sins—is actually an instrument of shame, because it demeans you for being human. It is one more example of the false identity inflicted on you by Christian theology that is held hostage by the doctrine of original sin.

A Better Mirror

Taken together, these moments of insight from two church services, persuaded me that most us of need a deeper vision of who we are than sin-soaked claims that we are sinners who need to be reminded again and again of our failures and faults and limitations. Most of us don't need to stare at our tiny images on the back of the spoon, the one that reflects an image defined by the doctrine of original sin. We need a better mirror.

There is no transformative power in telling you what is *wrong* with you. Transformative power comes from hearing what is *right* with you. That means looking inside the spoon, to see that your image of yourself is upside down.

The Gospel of Matthew can be such a mirror, if you can wipe off the sin juice, look inside, and see what it actually reveals to you about yourself.

Part Five

The Identity

Of Jesus

In Matthew

Chapter 14
The Gospel of Matthew
As an Identity Story

> An essential definition is one that designates that which makes a thing what it is and distinguishes that thing from all other things.
>
> Edward P. J. Corbett

What Is It?

The subject of the Gospel of Matthew is the identity of Jesus. But what is the Gospel of Matthew? The beginning point of any discussion is the question of definition. *What is it?* What is the essential definition that makes the Gospel of Matthew what it is? What is it that distinguishes it from all other things?

Is the Gospel of Matthew a historical narrative about an actual person? Is it a mythic story about a mythic character? Is it some of both?—some factual history and some myth?

History or Myth?

Another great disservice the Christian church has done to believers comes down to this question of definition. The overwhelming tendency of the church is to treat the Christian gospels as historical narratives about an actual person, while ignoring the connection of these narratives with myth.

Since the word *myth* has such negative connotations in our common speech, it's particularly important to ask the "what is it?" question about myth. In our era, myth has become synonymous with something that is untrue. A "myth" is a fairy tale, a made-up story, a lie. "Myths" are stories told by primitive people who weren't as smart as we are because they were actually stupid enough to believe that a chariot pulled the sun across the sky each day. To define myth this way is something like calling the Grand Canyon a big ditch.

Definitions of myth depend on who does the defining. In an article on myth, Mary Magoulick includes this insightful quotation from Gregory Schrempp:

> "Myth" refers to colorful stories that tell about the origins of humans and the cosmos. Attitudes towards myth vary greatly. Some regard it as a source of spiritual growth, while others see only falsehood. Some see in myth the distinct character of particular cultures, while others see universal patterns. Some regard myth as "contemporary" and "alive", while others think of it as "ancient" and/or "dead" (Schrempp).

These few words encompass the range of meanings contained within the word myth. Myth can be eternal truths or ignorant lies. The value of myth depends on who does the evaluation.

Meanwhile, the assessment of the Christian Gospels as history has something of an inverse relationship to myth. The more you consider the Gospels as history, the less you will see any connection to myth. The more you consider the Gospels as myth, the less you will see any connection to history.

The Historical Critical Method and the Rise of Fundamentalism

Starting in the nineteenth century, and continuing on into the twentieth, the preeminent method of biblical scholarship was the *historical critical method*. You see the word historical there? This is a clue that historical questions took priority. Historical criticism is a study of the development of the biblical texts themselves. The whole process could get very detailed—and very arcane—as scholars pored over biblical texts to decide what words and phrases and sentences came from what historical sources.

It was also an era in which archeologists discovered troves of significant ancient manuscripts and excavated ancient ruins. Scholars began to see the similarities between biblical writings and earlier traditions. In all of this, the predominant issues were historical issues. What were the historical connections between these ancient manuscripts and ruins and biblical writings? What was historically accurate? What was not historically accurate?

In response to this type of scholarly historical study, which began to challenge long-held beliefs about the Bible, some Christian believers reacted by insisting on the historical truth of *every* part of the Bible. Fundamentalism began in the late nineteenth century, but took hold as a movement in the early twentieth century. Contemporary Evangelicalism is an outgrowth of Fundamentalism. The predominant issues for both Fundamentalists and Evangelicals are also historical issues. Beliefs about inerrancy and infallibility are claims that the Bible is historically accurate in every way.

My point in all of this is that the questions that have defined much Bible study for the last hundred years are predominantly historical questions. In such an era, myth has received much less attention, either among biblical scholars or in churches.

The New Testament Gospels as Hero's Journey Stories

While biblical scholars and churches were involved in often hostile confrontations on historical questions, scholars in other fields were deeply involved in the study of ancient myths.

One of the best-known examples is Joseph Campbell. His book, *The Hero with a Thousand Faces,* first published in 1949, is a study of the *hero myth*. He demonstrated how this type of story has been known throughout human history, in all cultures. Campbell's outline of the hero's journey has become the story structure of many movies, including the biggest blockbuster movies.

All hero's journey stories are some form of salvation story, and all heroes are saviors. A hero is someone who saves someone or something from some sort of threat. Hero's journeys are not self-serving adventure stories, or stories of self-discovery, or stories about seeking rewards or treasure. Even though hero's journeys can be full of adventure and self-discovery and even treasure, the motive for the journey is salvation of others.

Every hero's journey is both an outer journey and an inner journey.

The *outer journey* is the mission of the hero. The hero sets out on a journey to end the threat to the hero's world. Hero's journeys involve a change in geography, as the hero leaves home and goes to the location of the threat's greatest power. There, the successful hero must confront the threat and defeat it to end the threat.

The *inner journey* concerns the inner struggles of the hero. The hero doesn't start out as a hero. Hero's journeys are about ordinary people who become heroes by the journey itself. Every hero must undergo some sort of death of the former self to become the savior.

The Gospels as Hero's Journey Stories

The hero's journey is the story structure of the four New Testament Gospels. Even the name *Jesus* means *savior*. This means that each of the New Testament Gospels shares themes, motifs, and events common in other ancient mythic stories.

The essential question is: If these gospel stories are hero's journeys, who or what needs to be saved from what threat? Are they really stories about how Jesus had to die on the cross to save you from your sinful nature?

My premise is that this salvation doctrine misses the essential meanings of these biblical hero's journey stories, which the Christian church calls Gospels. Here, we will look at only one of the four Gospel stories, the Gospel of Matthew. Why choose Matthew's Gospel? It's because the Gospel of Matthew is the clearest *whole story* about salvation for innocent victims of abuse anywhere in the Bible.

The Hero's Journey of Jesus in the Gospel of Matthew

Matthew's Gospel is a textbook example of the hero's journey story structure. If we read the Gospel of Matthew as a hero's journey rather than a morality tale about a perfect savior, we can see something in the story that most of us have never seen before. Jesus has to do what all heroes do. He has to learn how to be a savior by going on his own hero's journey.

In Matthew's Gospel, both the outer and inner journeys of Jesus are about his own identity. The Gospel of Matthew begins with the fundamental claim of the book. Jesus is the Messiah—the Christ—the son of David, the son of Abraham.

Matthew's purpose is to persuade readers that Jesus is the Messiah by telling a hero's journey story about Jesus. But the heroic story itself has to demonstrate another persuasive process. It has to show Jesus being persuaded that he is the Messiah.

Jesus has to become a hero the way all heroes become heroes. He has to go through an inner journey as well as an outer journey before he can truly become the Messiah. That is the essence of the hero's journey in Matthew. Jesus first has to believe that he is the Messiah in order to do what the Messiah does.

This is what all hero's journey stories have to do. Before they tell what the hero does, they have to show what the hero has to go through to do it. And "going through it" is not just a matter of facing outer obstacles. Every hero has to deal with inner obstacles of doubt, anxiety, reluctance, and fear.

The great advantage of looking at the Gospel of Matthew as a hero's journey is that it requires us to look first at Jesus as a human being. Christian theology claims that Jesus is both fully divine and fully human, but the human Jesus tends to get lost in the perfection of the divine Jesus.

If we can't see his humanity, we can't see the heroism of the story. And if we can't see the hero's journey of Jesus in Matthew, we can't see the Gospel of Matthew as model for our own heroic journeys to claim our true identities.

Journeys about Growth

Here's the most important point in all of this. Hero's journeys are not about magic transformations. They are about growth.

The ordinary person at the beginning of the story is capable of becoming the hero at the end, but doesn't know it yet. In other words, the hero's journey is a story about how to turn what is potential into what is actual.

This more than anything else is why the hero's journey is a type of story that has existed for as long as people have told stories. The story form itself tells of ordinary people who become more than they thought they were capable of being, by doing what they thought they were not capable of doing. Hero stories inspire us to look within for strength, courage, and resolve.

If you read the Gospel of Matthew as a believer, from the perspective of Christian piety, you know at the outset that Jesus is the Messiah—the Christ. Therefore, it ought to be obvious to everyone else in the story, including Jesus. If you read it that way, Jesus has no need to grow in his own consciousness about his true identity and no need to let go of any traces of false identity that might stop him from claiming his true identity.

But if you read it as the story of a hero, you can see that Jesus has to do what every hero has to do. He has to become a hero. To become a hero, he has to see himself capable of becoming a hero.

Chapter 15
The Identity of the Messiah

Shallow understanding from people of good will is more frustrating than absolute misunderstanding from people of ill will.

Martin Luther King, Jr.

Messiah, Kingdom of Heaven, Satan

Before we get to the story itself, the Gospel of Matthew concerns three loaded theological terms from Hebraic religious traditions:

- messiah

- kingdom of heaven

- Satan

If you ask many Christian Bible readers what these terms mean, they will probably say that: The Messiah is the same as the Christ. The kingdom of heaven means heaven. Satan is the devil who rules hell. This means that Jesus Christ is the savior whose atoning death on the cross saves humanity into an afterlife in heaven instead of eternal torment in hell.

If you could ask Matthew what he meant by these three terms, he would have dramatically different explanations. And these differences are the problem. If you don't understand what Matthew means by these terms, you don't understand the whole story as Matthew intended it, in its Whole Story context.

Who Rules the Earth?

Messiah, *kingdom of heaven*, and *Satan* are complex ideas in Hebrew traditions. However, Matthew's use of the terms is clear. In simplest terms, the common theme of these three terms concerns rulership of the earth.

Satan

According to Matthew's worldview, *Satan* is the *accuser*, the current and temporary ruler of the earth. Satan is not the polar opposite of God. God and Satan are not some sort of equally balanced yin and yang. For Matthew, God is all-powerful. Satan only rules on earth as long as God allows it.

Messiah

The *messiah* is the anticipated ruler who will save human beings from the rulership of Satan on earth. In Hebrew, messiah means *anointed one*. Anointing is a ritual that conveys authority. The messiah will have the authority to institute God's full reign on earth. This means that *messiah* is a royal title.

Kingdom of Heaven

The *kingdom of heaven* refers to earth under the rule of God's chosen king—the messiah. The kingdom of heaven is not about an afterlife in heaven.

Many biblical scholars argue that the language of "kingdom" is problematic here, because kingdom conveys the idea of a location. They argue that a much better translation would be "the rule of God" rather than "the kingdom of God. Although I agree with this argument, I will continue to use the kingdom language to be consistent with the translations I cite here.

Christ

I would be remiss to move on here without mentioning the significance of the word *christos*. Both *messiah* and *christ* are words with very deep and very complicated meanings in the ancient world and in the Bible. Matthew's Gospel was written in Greek and uses the word *christos* in 1:1 to identify Jesus. English Bibles translate *christos* as messiah or christ.

This need to make this translation choice raises important questions: Do *messiah* and *christ* share equivalent meanings? What did *messiah* mean in Hebraic traditions? What did *christos* mean in Greek, Jewish, and Christian traditions?

A related translation issue concerns capitalization. Are these general terms or specific titles? Is it Messiah or messiah? Christ or christ? Kingdom or kingdom? These are actually difficult translation choices in biblical translations. It's also difficult to decide whether or not to capitalize these designations in this brief overview.

In *The Pagan Christ*, Tom Harpur makes the case that the *christos myth* is the central concept of *every* ancient religion. For Harpur, the stories of Jesus are not about the one and only *Christ* but stories about *a* christ undergoing the familiar heroic journey of the *christos* myth:

> The ancients placed at the myth's centre an ideal person who would symbolize humanity itself in its dual nature of human and divine. This ideal person— the names were Tammuz, Adonis, Mithras, Dionysus, Krishna, Christ, and many others—symbolized the divine spark incarnate in every human being, the elements destined ultimately to deify humankind (Harpur 22).

Questions about the meanings of *messiah* and *christos* go far beyond the scope of *Your True Self Identity*, but they are significant questions for coming to terms with the relationship between history and myth in the Gospel stories of the New Testament.

Matthew's Worldview

The critical point in all of this is that the organizing principle of Matthew's worldview is that the messiah is the king who will overthrow Satan's rule on earth (the kingdom of the world) to inaugurate God's rule on earth (the kingdom of heaven).

This means that Matthew's gospel is fundamentally a hero's journey of the messiah who challenges the rule of Satan on earth. The unifying theme of the story is the critical idea: *the kingdom of heaven is near*.

It's also significant to note that everyone in the story shares the same worldview. His disciples, and the crowds who follow Jesus, as well as his adversaries, all know about the prophecies of the messiah. They all recognize the connection between the preaching of Jesus and messianic claims.

Son of God and Son of Man

In addition to the claim that Jesus is the Messiah/Christ (*messiah/christos*), Matthew identifies Jesus as both the "Son of God" and the "Son of Man." These are two more theologically loaded terms, which are also difficult to translate. Even deciding whether or not to capitalize these terms can be a difficult decision.

Hebrew often formed an adjective by using *son of* with a noun. Grammatically, *son of god* and *son of man* are parallel constructions. This means that *son of god* and *son of man* can function simply as adjectives. Used this way, *son of god* means *divine* and *son of man* means *human*. These are adjectival descriptions, not identity titles.

However, to treat each as simply an adjectival description doesn't do justice to the significance of these terms in Hebraic and early Christian theology.

Christian tradition uses the *Son of God* language as a unique identity claim about Jesus, to claim that Jesus is the one and only Son of God, despite the fact that the ancient world typically used son of god language to refer to kings and heroes, as well as human beings who became divine.

The Son of Man language also has deeply-rooted meanings in Jewish and Christian messianic expectations. It comprises various traditions about the Davidic king, the *chosen servant* language of Isaiah, and the vision of the *son of man* in Daniel 7.

The reference in Daniel 7 is worth citing here, because it still plays an important role in Christian messianic expectations of the "End Times."

In this case, I cite the King James Version rather than the New Revised Standard Version. Although the NRSV uses "Son of Man" language in Matthew, it uses "human being" language in Daniel. In Daniel, the phrase itself is in Aramaic rather than Hebrew:

> I saw in the night visions, and, behold, [one] like the Son of man came with the clouds of heaven, and came to the Ancient of days, and they brought him near before him. And there was given him dominion, and glory, and a kingdom, that all people, nations, and languages, should serve him: his dominion [is] an everlasting dominion, which shall not pass away, and his kingdom [that] which shall not be destroyed (Daniel 7:13-14, KJV).

In the first century of the Christian era, both the *son of man* language and the *messiah* language were well-known. In broad terms, messiah language referred to the role of the expected messiah as the eternal *ruler* of the kingdom of heaven on earth. In contrast, the son of man language referred to the role of the expected one as a *judge*. He is the one who will judge the kings, the princes, the rich, and the powerful, because they are the ones who have caused persecution and suffering of the vulnerable.

Translation Choices

This leads to the translation problems involved in conveying the meaning of these terms in translations. Translations consistently refer to Jesus as the Son of God. When it comes to the Son of Man language, some translations use "Son of Man." Some use the adjectival sense of "human being."

The NRSV uses "Son of Man," which maintains the parallel construction of Son of God. The CEB uses "Human One," which emphasizes the humanity of Jesus.

This is what the CEB says about their translation decisions concerning both the Hebrew and Greek terms:

> First, *ben 'adam* (Hebrew) or *huios tou anthropou* (Greek) are best translated as "human being" (rather than "son of man") except in cases of direct address, where CEB renders "Human" (instead of "Son of Man" or "Mortal," e.g., Ezek 2:1) (CEB, viii).

You see the problem. Even here, the CEB has to define both the simple adjectival use as "human being" and the use of the phrase as a direct address as "Human." (Actually, in the form of direct address, the CEB identifies Jesus as "the Human One.")

Chapter 16
The Identity of the "Real" Jesus

In religion and politics people's beliefs
and convictions are in almost every case
gotten at second-hand, and without
examination, from authorities who have
not themselves examined the questions
at issue but have taken them at second-
hand from others.

Mark Twain

Would the "Real" Jesus Say That?

The Son of Man language in the Gospel of Matthew is filled
with harsh language of judgment. The outright hostility of
Jesus in the Son of Man portions creates a problem for
some readers of the Gospel of Matthew. These readers
insist that the "real" Jesus would never say such things.
Therefore, all of the language of harsh judgment was added
by the writer of the Gospel of Matthew.

Stephen Mitchell argues for this position in *The Gospel
According to Jesus*:

> For all reputable scholars today acknowledge that
> the official Gospels were compiled, in Greek, many
> decades after Jesus' death, by men who had never
> heard his teaching, and that a great deal of what the
> "Jesus" of the Gospels says originated not in Jesus'
> own Aramaic words, which have been lost forever,
> but in the very different teachings of the early
> church. And if we often can't be certain of what he

said, we can be certain of what he didn't say"
(Mitchell 5).

Mitchell goes on to explain how "we can be certain of what
he didn't say":

> No careful reader of the Gospels can fail to be struck
> by the difference between the largeheartedness of
> such passages and the bitter, badgering tone of some
> of the passages added by the early church...

> Jesus teaches us, in his sayings and by his actions,
> not to judge (in the sense of condemn), but to keep
> our hearts open to all people; the later "Jesus" is the
> archetypal judge, who will float down terribly on the
> clouds for the world's final rewards and
> condemnations (Mitchell 8).

I include this material from Mitchell here to indicate that
the identity of Jesus as the Son of Man creates a problem
for anyone who believes that the "real" Jesus would never
judge anyone.

The Historical Jesus

I also include this material from Mitchell to demonstrate
once again the overwhelming influence of historical
thinking on the Bible. The distinction that Mitchell makes
between the "real" Jesus and the later "Jesus"
demonstrates his quest for the "historical" Jesus. At the
same time, his "historical" Jesus—the "real" Jesus—bears
striking resemblance to the "ideal persons" at the heart of
the *christos* myth.

In the same way, the *Jesus Seminar*, which attempts to
separate out the authentic words of Jesus from later
additions by the church, is on a quest to find the "historical"
Jesus. The "historical Jesus" of the Jesus Seminar was "an
itinerant Hellenistic Jewish sage and faith healer who

preached a gospel of liberation from injustice in startling parables and aphorisms" ("Jesus Seminar," *Wikipedia*).

The "Five Fundamentals" of Fundamentalism ("Fundamentalism," *Wikipedia*) are all resolutely historical in their claims about:

- the inspiration and inerrancy of the Bible

- the virgin birth of Jesus

- the death of Christ as the atonement for sin

- the bodily resurrection of Christ

- the historical reality of the miracles of Christ

The goal to find the truth about "the historical Jesus" unites Stephen Mitchell, the Jesus Seminar, and Fundamentalism in a common quest. However, their methods and assumptions do not lead to the same Jesus.

"Proving" History by Belief

As Mitchell himself demonstrates, the difference between the "real" Jesus and the later "Jesus" is often a matter of circular reasoning, based on your own beliefs about Jesus.

Mitchell begins his book by referring to the *Jefferson Bible* created by Thomas Jefferson. Jefferson used a razor blade to cut out what he thought were the authentic stories and words of Jesus from the King James Bible. He pasted these portions onto the pages of a blank book. He continued the project over several years. He also included the Greek text, and Latin and French translations of his selected verses. In the process, he created his own Bible, *The Life and Morals of Jesus of Nazareth* (Mitchell 3-4).

The Smithsonian published a full-color facsimile in November, 2011. It is also available as a public work and available on the internet (Jefferson).

What Jefferson did by hand, over years of his life, is what Christian churches and individual believers do by practice.

No church—even the churches that are most insistent that they live by the Word of God—treats every part of the Bible equally. Each builds its foundation on particular verses and books, while effectively ignoring the rest. This is why different denominations exist. They stake their claims on different terrain in the Bible.

Beyond Belief

The limitation of taking a razor blade to the Bible, whether it is a real blade or a metaphorical one, is that it does nothing to defuse the power of Bible in the hands of people who "believe" the parts of the Bible that you don't "believe." If all you have is your belief against someone else's belief, there's no way to move beyond stalemate.

For good or ill, the Gospel of Matthew, as it was written in Greek, is the story that the Christian church identifies as canonical scripture. This is the story the church claims as authoritative. And in this story, we do have Jesus talking about an archetypal judge "who will float down terribly on the clouds."

We ignore this material at our peril because others who do "believe" it are sure that Jesus is on their side. My goal is to give you some insights to move beyond such stalemates, so you have a solid foundation to stand on when you come face to face with people who cite the Bible to rob you of your freedoms.

Myth, History, and Persuasion

My goal is to read the Gospel of Matthew as a whole story that is both historical and mythic. However, my approach to both history and myth is not about the endless quest to separate out the "historical Jesus" from the "mythical Christ."

Instead, my focus is on the Gospel of Matthew as a story written to persuade. In this story, the author of the story used well-known Whole Story myths to accomplish a persuasive agenda in a historical setting. The primary myth is the hero's journey. The historical setting is first century Palestine during the era of Roman occupation.

Chapter 17
Identities of "The Little Ones" and
The Elites

> The fact of inequality is almost surely as old as the human species. No known society has ever had a completely egalitarian social system.
>
> Gerhard E. Lenski

The Bible Wasn't Written for You

When it comes to the Bible, the tendency of the Christian church is to universalize what was particular. Books written for particular groups of people become books addressed to *everyone*.

Every biblical book was written by someone, in some context, for some persuasive purpose. However, when these individual books became part of the authoritative canon, they became *scripture*. When each of these individual scriptures are part of one book—The Bible—the *when* and *where* and *what* and *why* and *who* of each biblical book can easily get lost.

A significant part of this process of turning the particular into the universal concerns *time*. Every word in the Bible was written at a particular time. No one sat down in the ancient world to write something for people living two or three thousand years later. The Biblical books weren't written for you or me. They were written for people living in their own time, to address their problems.

Each biblical book was also written with some agenda. Writers write with the intention of persuading someone of something. When you write something for someone else to read, you have an intention behind it. You want to persuade your reader or hearer of something. It could be as simple as writing "happy birthday" on a card, or as deliberately persuasive as writing a manifesto about some highly charged political topic. You don't write anything for someone else to read if you don't want your reader to react in some way.

In the previous chapter, I argued that *history* is the common thread connecting people who hold widely different views about Jesus. A concern for historicity shapes the questions: Did Jesus really exist? What is the connection between the "real" Jesus and the "Jesus" of the Bible? Is "Jesus" simply the character name of a familiar ancient story about the *christos* myth?

My premise here is that such historical questions about Jesus divert attention from the persuasive purposes of the Gospel narratives themselves. In the Gospel of Matthew, the story is about Jesus as the savior of *the little ones*. Historical questions about whether or not Jesus existed cannot answer the obvious question: Who are the little ones and why do they need to be saved?

Who Gets What and Why?

To answer that question, we need to ask sociological questions about the society of first century Palestine. I became aware of the need to ask such questions because of one person who "held up a spoon" to the Bible and showed me a perspective that I had never seen before.

During my doctoral work, Dr. Marvin L. Chaney, Professor of Old Testament at the San Francisco

Theological Seminary—one of the member schools of the Graduate Theological Union—taught me to think about the Bible in sociological terms. My term for his impact on my perspective is: I became *chaneyized*. This chaneyized perspective changed forever the way I see, not only the Bible, but every story I read in the news about current economic, political, social, and religious issues.

Power and Privilege

Chaney himself was a student of Gerhard E. Lenski, whose masterwork, *Power and Privilege: A Theory of Social Stratification*, answers the question: Who gets what and why?

It describes how human societies become *stratified* into layers between social classes, with the *haves* on the top and the *have-nots* on the bottom. Social stratification is about who has power and who is powerless, who has privilege, and who hasn't. It's why the rich get richer and the poor get poorer. It explains why religion and politics are two sides of the same coin, a coin made of wealth, money, and power.

If sin theology is the filter that turns parabolic Gospel stories about abuse of power into morality tales about sinners, then rugged American individualism is the filter that turns parabolic Gospel stories about the savior of the little ones into morality tales about Jesus as your personal savior. At the same time, a "spiritual perspective" on the Jesus as the *christos* can easily lose the real world realities of social injustice and human suffering in *this* world.

Saving the Little Ones

In the Gospel of Matthew, Jesus sets out to save the little ones from the abuse of power by the elite. It's not a story about saving you from your sins. It's also not a spiritual story about the "cosmic Christ" who transcends all of the limitations of this world. Matthew draws on well-known mythic material to tell the story, but the story itself is deeply rooted in first century Palestine.

In the Gospel of Matthew, Jesus refers to *children*, *infants*, and *little ones*. All have one characteristic in common. They are powerless in the social structure:

- *Children* are powerless because they are below the age of majority and don't have the legal rights of adults, in the society of Jesus or in ours. They are dependent upon adults to take care of them.

- The designation, *infant*, includes babies and very young children, as well as the childlike. It also refers to a *minor* in the sense of someone who is not yet of legal age.

- The phrase *little ones* is derived from the adjective, *mikrós*, which means *small*. Small can refer to size, to age, and to self-esteem. It can also refer to social status, power, and influence.

The setting of the story is what sociologists call an *advanced agrarian* society, in which wealth and power are based on agriculture and land rather than money. It was also society with a *tributary mode of production*. In simple terms, this means that wealth moved upwards, from the little ones to the elite.

The Elites of Palestine

Herod Antipas

King Herod Antipas, the son of Herod the Great, claimed ownership of just about all of the land of Palestine as his property. He also claimed ownership of most of the Sea of Galilee. This claim was typical of rulers in agrarian societies throughout history, in every society in the world. At the same time, peasant families lived on their own ancestral land. Ownership of the land passed from father to eldest son and could not be *alienated* from the family by selling it to anyone outside the family.

How can both the king and peasant farmers own the same land? Lenski explains the seeming contradiction here by emphasizing that "property consists basically of rights, not of things":

> If this is true, then agrarian rulers are owners, or part owners, not only of their royal estates and other land which they lease, assign, or grant as fiefs, but also of all the lands from which they, by right, exact taxes or tribute—especially if they are free to use these revenues for private purposes. They are also, for the same reason, part owners of all the business enterprises they tax.
>
> Our modern difficulty in grasping the true nature of such taxes stems from our tendency to think of proprietary rights as somehow individual. Either the peasant-farmer owns the land or the king owns it; they cannot both own it at the same time" (Lenski 216).

Taxes

When you think about, it's not all that different from property ownership in our era. Even if you own your house and land outright, and have the deed to prove it, local government has the right to tax your property and will take possession if you do not pay your property taxes.

When it comes to paying taxes, the significant difference between an agrarian society and a capitalistic society is what you use to pay your taxes. You pay your property taxes with money. The peasant farmers paid taxes with a portion of their crops. Otherwise, what Benjamin Franklin said about death and taxes remains true:

> Our new Constitution is now established, and has an
> appearance that promises permanency; but in this
> world nothing can be said to be certain, except death
> and taxes (Benjamin Franklin, 1789).

Unless you are living as a hunter/gatherer, you are going to pay taxes to some authority.

According to Lenski, as soon as human societies settle down long enough to grow crops and begin to store any surplus for later, *social stratification* begins. Some people get more of the surplus and some people get less. This distribution of the surplus creates social classes. The greater the surplus, the greater the distance between the ones in the top layers and the ones in the bottom layers.

Since King Herod had the right of ownership of all of the land as well as the parts of the Sea of Galilee that bordered his kingdom, he had the right to collect rent and taxes from the peasant farmers in the form of a portion of their annual harvest. The portion could be as much as one-third of the crop. He also had the right to collect rent and taxes from the fishermen, in the form of a portion of the catch. The king claimed the right to a portion of anything that anyone *produced,* including crops grown on the land, animals from the herds, fish from the waters, and "things" made with your hands.

In addition, the king had the right to grant gifts of land to other members of the aristocracy. Then the peasant farmers owed additional rent and taxes, in the form of a portion of their crops to the elites in Jerusalem.

The system of rents and taxes didn't stop there, because the peasant farmers had to pay more taxes to the temple.

How Wealth Moved Upwards

The Temple

The temple system was at the heart of the whole system of moving wealth upwards. Think of the temple as a combined central bank, tax collector, debt collection agency, and wealth redistributor. It collected the rents and mandatory tithes from the lowest classes and redistributed them to the ruling aristocracy, the priesthood, and the whole system of government administrators.

Pontius Pilate

The temple also collected rents and taxes for the Romans. Palestine was under the iron-fisted rule of the Roman Empire. Herod Antipas was a client king of Rome, who ruled under the authority of Pontius Pilate, the Roman procurator of the province. Pontius flagrantly abused both Roman and Jewish law. He spent most of his time and effort amassing as much wealth as possible before he returned to Rome, where he could live out his days as a wealthy man.

The High Priest

After Pontius Pilate, the high priest was the most powerful man in Roman-occupied Palestine. He collaborated with Rome as he ruled over the chief priests and the Sanhedrin.

The Chief Priests

The chief priests functioned as the board of directors of the temple. They controlled the sale of animals for the daily sacrifices. They also controlled the treasury and collected the required taxes and tithes.

The chief priests distributed the wealth upwards from the ones who produced the crops and caught the fish and raised the livestock, to the ruling aristocracy, which included priests and government administrators.

The Sanhedrin

The Sanhedrin was the high council. It functioned as a legislative body—a Congress or Parliament—made up of both religious and secular leaders. It included chief priests, elders, and scribes.

Many of the members of the Sanhedrin were absentee landlords for the peasant farmers in rural areas. They charged exorbitantly high *rents* from the peasant farmers. Once again, it's important to recognize that property consists of rights, not things. The peasant farmers actually owned the "things"—the land itself—but the elites in Jerusalem owned the rights to the land. The elites used their rights to extract as much wealth as possible from their properties in rural areas.

The Scribes

The scribes were both secretaries and lawyers. They could write in a society in which most people were illiterate. They also were the official interpreters of the law.

The Little Ones

The Peasant Farmers

Under this tributary system, which moved wealth upwards, peasant farmers could pay as much as four-fifths of everything they produced as crops in the form of rents and taxes. These rents and taxes went to the ruling aristocracy and priesthood, and to the Roman procurator, by way of the temple system. In addition, the peasant farmers could be forced to do compulsory labor.

The result was that the peasant farmers on their own land lived in desperate poverty. If their crops failed, they could lose their family land because they could not pay the required taxes and rents.

The Artisans

As poor as the peasant farmers were, they were better off than the artisans. Artisans were workers skilled in a trade that was other than farming the land.

Most became artisans because they were not first-born sons. Ownership of the family property passed from father to first-born son, by the right of primogeniture. (Notice that this is another right to own property.) By law, the land could not be sold outside of the family. The land could not be divided up between sons. Daughters could not inherit land. This meant that additional sons in the family were disinherited. Sons without property became the artisans. Artisans were usually much poorer than the poor peasant farmers, and depended on the peasant farmers for work.

Incidentally, the Gospel of Mark identifies Jesus as a carpenter, and the Gospel of Matthew calls Joseph a carpenter. Carpenters were landless artisans, lower in social status than peasant farmers, and usually even poorer than the farmers who lived on the family land. Many artisans were too poor to marry.

The Degraded

But even the artisans were not the lowest of the low. Beneath the landless artisans, a large group of *degraded* people did the society's dirty work.

The religious system separated the *clean* from the *unclean*. Those who worked with animals, such as shepherds, were ritually unclean. The tanners who worked with animal hides were ritually unclean. Those who sold their bodies for sex were ritually unclean. In addition to shepherds, tanners, and prostitutes, this large group of unclean people included porters, burden bearers, miners, and others.

The Expendables

The lowest of the low were a large group of *expendables*. These were the unemployed and nonproductive people, the beggars, the thieves, the outlaws, the lepers, and others who were the outcast of the society. The expendables were the most deprived and most malnourished and the most dehumanized. They are the littlest of the little ones.

The Shocking Claim

The "spoon" that Jesus holds up again and again in the Gospel of Matthew is a shocking vision of turning an upside down world right side up. He proclaims that the little ones will enter the kingdom of heaven and the elites at the center of power in Jerusalem will not. As you can imagine, this was much more popular message for the little ones than it was for the elites in Jerusalem.

In the next four chapters, we'll look at significant moments in the hero's journey of Jesus. In the following episodes, Jesus must decide who he is, and what he is willing to do to be true to his own identities. It's a story in four parts, following Christopher Vogler's hero's journey structure, rather than the three-part structure of Joseph Campbell.

[Note to reader: Even though I will cite only a few episodes in the Gospel of Matthew, I urge you to read the whole of the Gospel of Matthew as one whole story.]

Part Six

Identity Questions

of

The Hero

Chapter 18
Identity Questions
Of a Fatherless Man

Stage One: Leaving the Ordinary World
Matthew 1:1-4:11

The value of identity, of course, is that
so often with it comes purpose.
Richard R. Grant

The Ordinary World

The first stage of a hero's journey introduces the hero in the hero's *ordinary world*. It shows the *call to adventure* to the hero's journey. The Gospel of Matthew is a bit unusual because it provides a lot of backstory about the hero before we meet the hero himself.

Who Am I?

The Gospel of Matthew begins with this statement:

An account of the genealogy of Jesus the Messiah, the son of David, the son of Abraham (Matthew 1:1, NRSV).

This statement is followed by a long list of names. This is the kind of boring trivia that you will find here and there in the Bible. It's easy to skip over this stuff. However, if all you see here is a boring list of names, you have already missed the motivating question for Jesus on his inner journey.

What is the purpose of the genealogy? Its apparent purpose is to prove that Jesus has the right ancestry to be the Messiah because he is a descendent of David, who is a descendent of Abraham.

Notice two details about this genealogy. The first detail is that this is not a complete family tree, because it traces ancestry through the fathers, not the mothers. It is a list of fathers of fathers of fathers of fathers of fathers, generation after generation of fathers.

What about the mothers? The genealogy mentions only four mothers: Rahab; Ruth; the wife of Uriah; and Mary. The most significant detail in this genealogy concerns Mary, the mother of Jesus. This is how the genealogy identifies Jesus:

> ...and Jacob the father of Joseph the husband of Mary, of whom Jesus was born, who is called the Messiah (Matthew 1:16, NRSV).

Who Is the Father of Jesus?

In this long list of fathers and sons, Jesus is the only one whose father is not named.

If the purpose of the genealogy is to prove that Jesus has the right paternal ancestry to be the Messiah, we have a problem. Joseph is the husband of Mary, who is the mother of Jesus, but Joseph is not named as the father of Jesus. All Matthew has demonstrated is that Joseph has the right ancestry to be the Messiah, but Jesus doesn't.

If you assume that Matthew was a careful writer, who knew exactly what he was doing, you then have to ask another question. What is the function of this genealogy in the Gospel of Matthew? Why begin the book with a boring genealogy and then immediately use the genealogy itself as evidence against your own claim?

This apparent genealogical contradiction lays the foundation for two identity claims about Jesus in the Gospel of Matthew. Matthew says that Jesus is the Messiah but he is not the son of Joseph. This raises the significant question: Who is the father of Jesus?

Matthew answers this question immediately by stating that the father of Jesus is the Holy Spirit. Jesus is the Son of God:

> Now the birth of Jesus the Messiah took place in this way. When his mother Mary had been engaged to Joseph, but before they lived together, she was found to be with child from the Holy Spirit (Matthew 1:18, NRSV).

A Story about a Man without a Father

Although the idea of a virgin mother gets most of the attention, in Matthew, the real story that Matthew intends to tell is not about the maternity of Jesus, but about his paternity.

Everything that Matthew includes about the birth of Jesus—the genealogy, the story about the virgin birth, and the visit of the wise men to Herod—concerns paternity.

If we can put theological claims and historical questions aside and read the Gospel of Matthew simply as a story, we can see a man with an identity problem.

Ancient Israel was a patriarchal society. Men were identified by their fathers. You can see it in the genealogy, which identifies generations of men in terms of their fathers. Jesus sticks out like a sore thumb because he is the only man identified only by his mother.

The family structure in ancient Israel was organized around the father as the *head of the household*. In Hebrew, *beth 'ab* means *house of the father*. Families lived as multigenerational units on the family's property, under the authority of the eldest male.

The firstborn son of a family would inherit the family's property. Younger sons would continue to live on the family's ancestral property under the authority of the older brother, or they could become landless artisans. But a man without a father had no rightful place and no rightful inheritance. He had no legitimate identity.

A Journey about Identity

If we are going to read the Gospel of Matthew as a story, without first filtering the story through Christian theological claims and beliefs about Jesus, we need to consider the situation as Matthew lays it out before us.

We have a story about a man who has no earthly father. The story says at the outset that Jesus is both the Messiah and the Son of God, but that doesn't mean that Jesus knew that he was both the Messiah and the Son of God.

The Gospel of Matthew is a story about a man who is on a journey to discover and claim his identity as the Son of God. In a society in which men were known by their fathers, the inner question motivating his hero's journey is this: Who am I if I don't know the identity of my father?

He has to undergo the hero's journey to discover that he is the Son of God, and more importantly, to *believe* that is his true identity. It is only when he fully claims his identity as the Son of God that he can fully claim his identity as the Messiah.

This means that the central theme of the hero's journey of Jesus in the Gospel of Matthew is the identity of Jesus. You will also see that it is not an easy journey. The journeys of heroes never are.

What follows are significant moments in the story when Jesus himself must come to terms with his own identity.

The Baptism of Jesus

We first meet Jesus as a character in the story when he comes to be baptized by John:

> Then Jesus came from Galilee to John at the Jordan, to be baptized by him. John would have prevented him, saying, "I need to be baptized by you, and do you come to me?" But Jesus answered him, "Let it be so now; for it is proper for us in this way to fulfill all righteousness." Then he consented (Matthew 3:13-15, NRSV).

After the baptism, Jesus has this significant experience:

> And when Jesus had been baptized, just as he came up from the water, suddenly the heavens were opened to him and he saw the Spirit of God descending like a dove and alighting on him. And a voice from heaven said, "This is my Son, the Beloved, with whom I am well pleased" (Matthew 3:16-17, NRSV).

This is the first time in the story that Jesus hears directly from God that he is God's son. Not only that, he hears that he is "Beloved" and that his father is "well pleased" with him.

This baptism experience is rich with meaning in the ancient world. Kings were often baptized before they assumed the throne, and kings were often identified as the Son of God.

Confirmation of Two Identities

Significantly, the baptism of Jesus answers the two significant questions of his hero's journey.

The first question is the outer question asked by everyone Jesus encounters on his journey. Is Jesus the

Messiah? Is he the long-awaited king who will usher in the kingdom of God—the rule of God—on earth?

The second question is the inner question of Jesus himself: Who am I, if I don't have a father?

From the perspective of the inner journey of a man with questionable paternity and without a father's name in his genealogy, these words answer the fundamental question of his life: Who is my father?

This is how the hero's journey begins for Jesus. It begins with a confirmation of two identities. He is both the Messiah and the Beloved Son of God. And most significantly, the confirmation comes as a declaration of a father's love for his son.

The First Test

After the baptism, Jesus is led into the wilderness for his first test:

> Then Jesus was led up by the Spirit into the wilderness to be tempted by the devil. He fasted forty days and forty nights, and afterwards he was famished (Matthew 4:1-2, NRSV).

Temptation One: Food

The devil's first temptation takes the form of a taunt concerning Jesus' identity as the Son of God. The devil says, "If you are the Son of God, command these stones to become loaves of bread":

> The tempter came and said to him, "If you are the Son of God, command these stones to become loaves of bread." But he answered, "It is written, 'One does not live by bread alone, but by every word that comes from the mouth of God" (Matthew 4:3-4, NRSV).

In other words: If you really are the Son of God, you can do anything. You can use your powers to get what you want. You can satisfy your hunger after a forty-day fast by turning stones into bread.

The essential test here is whether Jesus will use his identity as the Son of God to get what he wants.

Temptation Two: Salvation

The second temptation by the devil uses the same strategy:

> Then the devil took him to the holy city and placed him on the pinnacle of the temple, saying to him, "If you are the Son of God, throw yourself down; for it is written, 'He will command his angels concerning you,' and 'On their hands they will bear you up, so that you will not dash your foot against a stone.'" Jesus said to him, "Again it is written, 'Do not put the Lord your God to the test'" (Matthew 4:5-7, NRSV).

This time, the devil uses the same formula: "If you are the Son of God, throw yourself down." If Jesus is really the Son of God, angels will come to save him, even if he jumps off the highest point of the temple. Jesus will hear similar taunts again when he is hanging on the cross (Matthew 27:39-44).

Once again, Jesus tells the devil that he will not protect his life by using his identity as the Son of God to test God.

Temptation Three: Authority to Rule

In the third temptation, the devil takes a different tack:

> Again, the devil took him to a very high mountain and showed him all the kingdoms of the world and their splendor; and he said to him, "All these I will give you, if you will fall down and worship me." Jesus said to him, "Away with you, Satan! For it is written,

> 'Worship the Lord your God, and serve only him'"
> (Matthew 4:8-10, NRSV).

This time, the temptation is not in terms of the identity of Jesus as the Son of God. He is now dealing with the identity of Jesus as the Messiah, the king who will overthrow Satan's rule on earth (the kingdom of the world) to inaugurate God's rule on earth (the kingdom of heaven).

The devil offers Jesus the authority to rule all of the kingdom of the world if Jesus will renounce his identity as the Messiah. Jesus refuses to surrender his identity as the Messiah in exchange for earthly power.

The End of the First Test

Jesus passes the first test on his hero's journey, which demonstrates his willingness to accept his true identities as Messiah and Son of God:

> Then the devil left him, and suddenly angels came
> and waited on him (Matthew 4:11, NRSV).

These three temptations get to essence of every test Jesus will face on his hero's journey. At every stage of his journey, these two questions about his identity define his journey:

- Outer question: Are you the Messiah?

- Inner question: Am I truly the Beloved Son of God?

Chapter 19
Identity Tests
with
Allies and Adversaries

Stage Two: The Road of Trials
Matthew 4:12-17:13

It is surmounting difficulties that makes heroes.

Louis Pasteur

Leaving Home

After this testing of his willingness to accept the call to adventure of his hero's journey, Jesus is now ready to leave home.

In this stage of the journey, the hero crosses a geographical boundary dividing the hero's *ordinary world* from what Joseph Campbell called *the special world of the adventure*. Vogler calls this part of the journey the *Road of Trials,* when Jesus will undergo more tests of his identities.

The ordinary world of Jesus is his hometown of Nazareth in Galilee. This Road of Trials begins when he leaves Nazareth and goes to the nearby Galilean city of Capernaum (Matthew 4:13).

To fulfill his mission as the Messiah, Jesus must go south to Judea, to confront the power of the temple and monarchy in Jerusalem. But in this stage of his journey, Jesus stays in the north. His travels take him throughout Galilee and to Gentile areas on the eastern side of the Sea of Galilee and north into Syria. At this stage of his journey, Jesus is not ready to go to Jerusalem.

Most heroes are reluctant at first. Even when they begin the journey in the special world of adventure, they are not fully committed to the journey. Although Matthew doesn't describe the kind of inner conflict in Jesus that Augustine reveals about himself, the story itself demonstrates that Jesus does not rush headlong into the mission.

Proclaiming the Good News of the Kingdom

At this stage of his journey, Jesus proclaims the *good news* of the kingdom of heaven close to home:

> Then Jesus went about all the cities and villages, teaching in their synagogues, proclaiming the good news of the kingdom, and curing every disease and every sickness. When he saw the crowds, he had compassion for them, because they were harassed and helpless, like sheep without a shepherd (Matthew 9:35-36, NRSV).

Jesus also gathers allies as he calls disciples to follow him.

Adversaries Accuse Jesus of Blasphemy

Adversaries first appear in the story in Chapter 9. In this case, the adversaries are scribes. Scribes are the official interpreters of the law.

Although Jesus rarely speaks in terms of forgiveness of sins in Matthew, in this case he tells a paralytic that his sins are forgiven:

> And after getting into a boat he crossed the sea and came to his own town. And just then some people were carrying a paralyzed man lying on a bed. When Jesus saw their faith, he said to the paralytic, "Take heart, son; your sins are forgiven." Then some of the scribes said to themselves, "This man is blaspheming" (Matthew 9:1-3, NRSV).

There are a several significant details here. First, this is the first evidence of the adversaries on his Road of Trials. These scribes believe that Jesus has committed *blasphemy* by forgiving sins, because only God can forgive sins.

Blasphemy is a serious charge. It refers to slander, cursing, or showing contempt for God. This first encounter with adversaries is a foreshadowing of things to come. At his trial, Jesus will be found guilty of blasphemy and sentenced to death.

Claiming Authority

This encounter also concerns *authority*, which is another term that recurs in Jesus' encounters with the adversaries. Throughout the Gospel of Matthew, the crowds marvel at his authority, and the adversaries challenge his authority:

> Then some of the scribes said to themselves, "This man is blaspheming." But Jesus, perceiving their thoughts, said, "Why do you think evil in your hearts? For which is easier, to say, 'Your sins are forgiven,' or to say, 'Stand up and walk'? But so that you may know that the Son of Man has authority on earth to forgive sins" --he then said to the paralytic-- "Stand up, take your bed and go to your home." And he stood up and went to his home. When the crowds saw it, they were filled with awe, and they glorified God, who had given such authority to human beings (Matthew 9:3-8, NRSV).

The Son of Man

This first encounter with adversaries also introduces another identity for Jesus. When Jesus speaks to adversaries about himself, he refers to himself as the *Son of Man*. The Son of Man is the one who will judge the kings, the princes, the rich, and the powerful, because they are the ones who have caused persecution and suffering of the vulnerable.

The reason that Jesus receives the death penalty comes down to his identity claim that he is the Son of Man, which gives him the right to judge the ones who are judging him.

The Road of Trials stage is about Jesus' growing fame and the growing opposition from his adversaries, as well as his separation from his ordinary world. Although every experience concerns his identity as Messiah, we'll look at only two significant moments at the end of the Road of Trials. These are the experiences that Campbell identified as the *approach to the inmost cave* and the *ordeal*.

In hero's journeys, geography and location matter. The ordeal experience usually occurs in some location that is extreme in some way. It can be very high, very low, very dark, very deep. The most common location in hero's journey stories is a cave or cave-like place—the *inmost cave*.

The ordeal is the *central event of the story* because it is the point of greatest change. Something in the hero must die for the hero to complete the journey. This is the point of crisis.

Crisis is another English word taken directly from Greek. The noun is *krísis*. The root meaning is *separation*. The crisis point separates a story into two halves, because it is the place where the hero undergoes some sort of permanent separation from the past.

Who Do You Say That I Am?

In this story, the approach to the inmost cave occurs in Caesarea Philippi. Geographically, Caesarea Philippi is north of Galilee, in an area filled with ancient temples to other gods. The place name was derived from a temple built by Herod the Great, which was dedicated to Caesar. Later, Herod's son Philip added his own name.

This means that Jesus was in a Gentile area, as far away from Jerusalem as he ever gets in the story, in an area filled with temples and monuments to gods and kings.

For the first time in the story, Jesus asks his disciples about his identity:

> Now when Jesus came into the district of Caesarea Philippi, he asked his disciples, "Who do people say that the Son of Man is?" And they said, "Some say John the Baptist, but others Elijah, and still others Jeremiah or one of the prophets." He said to them, "But who do you say that I am?" Simon Peter answered, "You are the Messiah, the Son of the living God" (Matthew 16:13-16, NRSV).

Three identities of Jesus come together in this one reference. In Matthew, Jesus often refers to himself as the Son of Man. Here, Peter identifies Jesus as both the Messiah and the Son of God.

This is Jesus' response to Peter:

> And Jesus answered him, "Blessed are you, Simon son of Jonah! For flesh and blood has not revealed this to you, but my Father in heaven (Matthew 16:17, NRSV).

This answer makes clear that Jesus himself has accepted his identities as Messiah and the Son of God.

Now that his disciples recognize Jesus as both the Messiah and the Son of God, Jesus does something else that he has not done before this. He begins to tell his disciples what is coming in his journey:

> Then he sternly ordered the disciples not to tell anyone that he was the Messiah. From that time on, Jesus began to show his disciples that he must go to Jerusalem and undergo great suffering at the hands of the elders and chief priests and scribes, and be killed, and on the third day be raised (Matthew 16: 20-22, NRSV).

Significantly, this willingness to go to Jerusalem, even though he knows he will be killed, means that Jesus is ready to face another type of death in the ordeal.

Tempted to Abandon the Journey

A critical test to his identities as the Messiah and Son of God comes at a stage in the journey that corresponds with what Campbell calls "Woman as Temptress." This is one of those places where Campbell's own categories can obscure a significant transitional point in the journey. Although the heroes in Campbell's *The Hero With A Thousand Faces* are all male, hero's journeys are not limited to males, and tempters who urge heroes to abandon their journeys don't have to be female:

> And Peter took him aside and began to rebuke him, saying, "God forbid it, Lord! This must never happen to you." But he turned and said to Peter, "Get behind me, Satan! You are a stumbling block [*skándalon*] to me; for you are setting your mind not on divine things but on human things" (Matthew 16:22-23, NRSV).

After calling Jesus the Messiah, the Son of the living God, Peter is unwilling to accept that Jesus must undergo death in Jerusalem.

Clearly, Peter is not a woman but he is a tempter here. Jesus calls Peter "Satan" because Peter is challenging Jesus just as Satan did in the wilderness temptations. In essence, Peter is making the same argument that Satan made: "If you are the Son of God, this cannot happen to you. God will not allow this to happen to his Son."

Jesus rejects this argument by Peter just as he rejected the argument by Satan.

Also, notice the NRSV language of "stumbling block" here. Once again, translations obscure the Greek meaning of *skándalon* as *trap*, by turning a trap into a "stumbling block." It is much more powerful to translate *skándalon* as trap, to have Jesus say: "Get behind me, Satan! You are a trap to me."

Matthew makes clear that Jesus is willing to do what his hero's journey requires of him. The last thing heroes need on their journeys is to have their closest allies hold them back just when they are ready to go the distance.

The Ordeal

This leads to the ordeal. Volger explains the ordeal this way:

> The Ordeal in myths signifies the death of the ego. The hero is now fully part of the cosmos, dead to the old, limited vision of things and reborn into a new consciousness of connections (Vogler 177).

In this crisis at the midpoint of the journey, the person who started out on the journey undergoes some sort of "death" of the former self. This death of the former self is the necessary impetus to continue the journey to the final confrontation with the ultimate adversary at the climax of the story.

Instead of a cave, the death experience of Jesus at the midpoint of the story takes place on a "high mountain."

Campbell has several terms for what happens at the midpoint of the story. The one that is most relevant for this story is *apotheosis*. This is another Greek word. It means to *deify*. In this story, the ordeal is the experience Christian tradition calls the *transfiguration:*

> Six days later, Jesus took with him Peter and James and his brother John and led them up a high mountain, by themselves. And he was transfigured [*metamorphóō*] before them, and his face shone like the sun, and his clothes became dazzling white. Suddenly there appeared to them Moses and Elijah, talking with him. Then Peter said to Jesus, "Lord, it is good for us to be here; if you wish, I will make three dwellings here, one for you, one for Moses, and one for Elijah" (Matthew 17:1-4, NRSV).

The Greek word translated as "transfigured" here is another word that has passed directly from Greek into English. It is *metamorphosis*, a word that means *change in form*.

Once again, Jesus hears the words he heard at his baptism:

> While he was still speaking, suddenly a bright cloud overshadowed them, and from the cloud a voice said, "This is my Son, the Beloved; with him I am well pleased; listen to him!" (Matthew 17:5, NRSV).

This time, the voice from the cloud includes these additional words, "listen to him." These are words conveying authority to Jesus.

Unlike the baptism, this time Jesus has witnesses. This is also characteristic of the ordeal at the midpoint of the journey. In many hero's journey stories, the hero's allies see the "death" experience and are frightened:

> When the disciples heard this, they fell to the ground and were overcome by fear. But Jesus came and

touched them, saying, "Get up and do not be afraid."
And when they looked up, they saw no one except
Jesus himself alone (Matthew 17:6-8, NRSV).

What Is the Metamorphosis?

What is the metamorphosis in this story? What changed in
Jesus? The story says that his face shone like the sun and
his clothes became dazzling white. This description is
similar to the description of the angel who rolled back the
stone after the resurrection of Jesus:

> And suddenly there was a great earthquake; for an
> angel of the Lord, descending from heaven, came
> and rolled back the stone and sat on it. His
> appearance was like lightning, and his clothing white
> as snow (Matthew 28:2-3, NRSV).

In the transfiguration experience, Jesus once again hears
that he is the Son of God. This time his divine nature
becomes visible. This is when it's worth remembering that
the construction *son of god* as an adjective means *divine*.
Jesus becomes the *Divine One*.

At the midpoint of the hero's journey, Jesus becomes
what Campbell calls the Master of Two Worlds. He is both
the Divine One and the Human One, the Son of God and
the Son of Man. This metamorphosis experience is the
essence of the *christos* myth described by Tom Harpur in
The Pagan Christ:

> ...the single vast theme (in fact, the central teaching)
> of all religions is indeed the incarnation of the divine
> in the human. Moreover, while the sun is the source
> of all that is in our solar system, it is also by its light
> alone that we are able to see and know everything
> that exists, and for that reason, it was a natural
> symbol in antiquity for the ultimate being, for God.
> Thus the radiant figure of the sun god, who really

> represented at the same time both the divine and
> also humanity divinized, was at the core of the
> Christos mythos in ancient times (Harpur 21).

Jesus becomes the radiant being who is both divine and
divinized human. This episode at the midpoint of the
journey is clear evidence of myth in the Gospel of Matthew.

What Changed in Jesus?

At the same time, what really changed in Jesus? James
Ryan argues against Campbell's idea that heroes
experience transformative changes, to become what they
had not been before:

> What does happen in any good story is not that
> characters change, but rather, their circumstances
> have forced them to take a new tack, and parts of
> their character that were previously dormant,
> suddenly open up and are revealed (Ryan 34).

This claim by Ryan is a liberating insight into what it takes
to become what you already are. In Matthew's story of
Jesus, Jesus didn't have to become the Son of God in a
deification process. He was born the Son of God.

The story of Matthew, read as a story, demonstrates
that it takes time and experiences for Jesus to claim his
identity. The experience of metamorphosis at the midpoint
of the journey comes after he has been tested on his
journey. At his baptism, he had not yet started his journey.
This time, when he again hears the words, "This is my Son,
my Beloved," he has earned his battle scars. This time,
witnesses hear the words of his identity. They also hear the
words affirming his authority to speak.

After all that he has endured so far on his journey,
Jesus is now ready to change direction and go to Jerusalem,
knowing that he will eventually die an actual death
because of his confrontation with the ultimate adversary.

His true identity did not change in the transfiguration experience. Only his perception of his identity changed. And because of this change, he is ready to become much more aggressive about claiming his true identities as the Messiah and the Son of God—the Divine One—and his identity as the Son of Man—the Divinized Human One.

Chapter 20
Claiming the Identity
of
The Messiah

Stage Three: The Reward
Matthew 17:4-26:45

> When we quit thinking primarily about
> ourselves and our own self-
> preservation, we undergo a truly heroic
> transformation of consciousness.
>
> Joseph Campbell

Changed Attitude

The third stage of the hero's journey is the *Reward*. It is both a time of reward for undergoing the "death" experience and of aggressive action by the hero to take something of value from the adversary.

You can see the change in Jesus after he comes down from the mountain. He becomes much more aggressive in his actions and words against his adversaries and more impatient with his disciples.

This changed attitude is directly related to the difference between most hero's journey stories and the hero's journey in Matthew's story. The death experience for Jesus at the midpoint of the journey is unlike the typical death experience of many hero's journey stories. In most hero's journey stories, the crisis at the midpoint is an encounter with an adversary and the death experience is the threat of actual physical death.

You already know what will happen to Jesus. He will die a real death, rather than a metaphorical death, in Jerusalem. When Jesus sets out for Jerusalem, he knows that he is going to die a horrible death.

Jesus makes clear by his words and actions that he is willing to die, but he doesn't want to. If you assert that Jesus was both fully human and fully God—as Christian theology proclaims—it's not difficult to see why Jesus becomes more impatient and exasperated with his disciples and more hostile to his adversaries.

Taking Possession

The unifying theme of the third stage of the hero's journey for Jesus is the theme of *possession*.

Although it might shock pious sensibilities to consider Jesus a thief, the intention of Jesus in this stage of the journey is to take away from his adversaries their most valuable possession. What is this possession? It is authority to rule earth.

The worldview underlying the Gospel of Matthew believes that the world is now under the temporary rulership of Satan and Satan's allies—the religious hierarchy and monarchy centered in Jerusalem. Jesus began his heroic mission by proclaiming the "good news of the kingdom." Everything that Jesus says or does in the Gospel of Matthew is rooted in the proclamation that "the kingdom of heaven is near."

Here, we will look at only two moments in this stage of the story, the entry into Jerusalem and the experience in Gethsemane.

Entering Jerusalem

After the transfiguration experience, Jesus and his disciples leave Galilee and make the trek south to Jerusalem. But when Jesus gets to Jerusalem, he doesn't simply walk into the city. He rides into Jerusalem on a donkey.

Although the Christian church treats the trial and crucifixion of Jesus as the unjust treatment of an innocent man, the Gospel of Matthew makes clear that Jesus was far from innocent. He deliberately provoked the religious and civic authorities. His ride into Jerusalem on a donkey was an act of asserting his identity as the Messiah. It was an overt claim of the right of possession.

The whole of Matthew's Gospel is set within a context in which everyone knew about the kingdom of heaven. Everyone knew that the Messiah was the king who would take rulership of earth away from Satan and Satan's allies.

Everything that Jesus does in Jerusalem is highly political and deliberately confrontational to both the Jewish religious and political leaders and to the Romans. At the time, Palestine was under the control of the Roman Empire and its brutal occupying force.

There is also nothing innocent about the timing. It was Passover, one of the major Jewish festivals. Significantly, Passover celebrates liberation from oppression in Egypt. The city of Jerusalem was packed with people who hated the Romans and wanted to be free of the occupiers.

Meanwhile, the religious leaders and the civic leaders of Jerusalem walked a fine line with the Romans. The Romans allowed the Jews to practice their religion. In return, the Romans would not tolerate any signs of rebellion. This means that the religious and civic leaders were on guard for any seditious actions that might provoke the Roman authorities.

So what does Jesus do? He rides into Jerusalem on a donkey. A man who walked everywhere didn't ride into Jerusalem because his feet hurt. He rode into Jerusalem because the prophet Zechariah (Zechariah 9:9) proclaimed that the Messiah would enter Jerusalem this way:

> This took place to fulfill what had been spoken through the prophet, saying, "Tell the daughter of Zion, Look, your king is coming to you, humble, and mounted on a donkey, and on a colt, the foal of a donkey." The disciples went and did as Jesus had directed them; they brought the donkey and the colt, and put their cloaks on them, and he sat on them (Matthew 21:4-7, NRSV).

The crowd knows exactly what this prophecy means. The Son of David is the Messiah, the king who is coming to overthrow the current rulers:

> A very large crowd spread their cloaks on the road, and others cut branches from the trees and spread them on the road. The crowds that went ahead of him and that followed were shouting, "Hosanna to the Son of David! Blessed is the one who comes in the name of the Lord! Hosanna in the highest heaven!" (Matthew 21:8-9, NRSV).

This flagrant, public act to claim his identity as the Messiah is a defiant political demonstration, packed with theological meaning. It is designed to rouse the crowds and aggravate the leadership.

The truth is that nothing Jesus does in Jerusalem is innocent. This includes the cleansing of the temple, his confrontations with the scribes, Pharisees, and Sadducees, and every parable he tells in this part of the journey. They are all defiant acts to claim the right of the Messiah to take possession of the rulership of earth, to bring in the rule of God in the kingdom of heaven on earth.

In addition to claiming his identity as the Messiah, Jesus also claims his identity as the Son of Man—the Human One—who claims the right to judge the rulers.

One example is the prophecy of the separation of the sheep and the goats. Although Christian tradition treats the shepherd metaphor as a sign of gentleness, the biblical metaphor is much less benign:

> Shepherds in the Bible were symbols of might, ferocity and royalty, whereas now they generally represent peaceful guidance and oversight. So the image of the Lord as shepherd in Psalm 23 originally meant that the Lord was mighty, fierce and royal. The impact was roughly the same as "the Lord is a man of war." But in most English-speaking cultures, "the Lord is my shepherd" conveys a wholly different, and therefore inaccurate, image (Hoffman).

There is nothing peaceful about the image of the Son of Man as the shepherd in the long prophecy in Matthew 25:31-46. Consider these excerpts as an example of Jesus in full Son of Man mode. (This is the kind of language that Mitchell attributes to the "Jesus" of the church, not the "real" Jesus.):

> When the Son of Man comes in his glory, and all the angels with him, then he will sit on the throne of his glory. All the nations will be gathered before him, and he will separate people one from another as a shepherd separates the sheep from the goats, and he will put the sheep at his right hand and the goats at the left. Then the king will say to those at his right hand, 'Come, you that are blessed by my Father, inherit the kingdom prepared for you from the foundation of the world' (Matthew 25:31-34).
>
> ...

> Then he will say to those at his left hand, 'You that
> are accursed, depart from me into the eternal fire
> prepared for the devil and his angels;...And these will
> go away into eternal punishment, but the righteous
> into eternal life (Matthew 25:41; 46, NRSV).

In response to these provocations, based on the two identities of the Messiah as the Son of God and the Judge as the Son of Man, the high priest Caiaphas, the chief priests, and the elders of the people decide to act against this dangerous provocateur, Jesus. But they are worried about causing a riot in the city crammed with Passover visitors:

> Then the chief priests and the elders of the people
> gathered in the palace of the high priest, who was
> called Caiaphas, and they conspired to arrest Jesus
> by stealth and kill him. But they said, "Not during the
> festival, or there may be a riot among the people"
> (Matthew 26:3-5, NRSV).

In contrast to these deliberately provocative acts to claim his outer identity as the Messiah, his experience in Gethsemane centers on the inner identity question of his hero's journey.

The Prayer in Gethsemane

> Then Jesus went with them to a place called
> Gethsemane; and he said to his disciples, "Sit here
> while I go over there and pray." He took with him
> Peter and the two sons of Zebedee, and began to be
> grieved and agitated. Then he said to them, "I am
> deeply grieved, even to death; remain here, and stay
> awake with me." And going a little farther, he threw
> himself on the ground and prayed, "My Father, if it is
> possible, let this cup pass from me; yet not what I
> want but what you want."

> Then he came to the disciples and found them sleeping; and he said to Peter, "So, could you not stay awake with me one hour? Stay awake and pray that you may not come into the time of trial; the spirit indeed is willing, but the flesh is weak."
>
> Again he went away for the second time and prayed, "My Father, if this cannot pass unless I drink it, your will be done." Again he came and found them sleeping, for their eyes were heavy.
>
> So leaving them again, he went away and prayed for the third time, saying the same words (Matthew 26-36-44, NRSV).

These are the words of a man who doesn't want to die.

This is the man without a human father who found his paternity in God. This is the man who heard two times—once at his baptism and once at his experience of transfiguration—that he is the Beloved Son of God.

But this time, no voice speaks from heaven. His Father does not speak. And unlike the Transfiguration, he has no witnesses. His disciples are sleeping. He is alone.

But despite silence from God, he is willing to do what he must do to fulfill his outer journey to claim his identities as the Son of God and the Son of Man.

Chapter 21
Identity of the Successful Hero

Stage Four: The Road Back
Matthew 26:46-28:20

A hero is someone who understands the responsibility that comes with his freedom.

Bob Dylan

Retaliation

The last stage of the hero's journey is the "Road Back." In the case of Jesus, the Road Back means returning to his ordinary world in Galilee. This is another turning point in the journey. Many hero's journey stories include another *death* experience at the climax of the journey, which results in an experience of *resurrection*.

In the Reward phase of his journey after the Transfiguration, Jesus claimed the right of possession in a very aggressive and confrontational manner. At the beginning of the Road Back stage of the journey, the adversaries strike back hard.

Since much of this story is familiar from church services, we'll look at only a few significant moments.

Are You the Messiah?

The first is his arrest in Gethsemane and his trial before the religious leaders in the middle of the night:

> Those who had arrested Jesus took him to Caiaphas
> the high priest, in whose house the scribes and the
> elders had gathered (Matthew 26:57, NRSV).

The purpose of the trial is to find evidence against Jesus to justify death:

> Now the chief priests and the whole council were
> looking for false testimony against Jesus so that they
> might put him to death, but they found none, though
> many false witnesses came forward. At last two
> came forward and said, "This fellow said, 'I am able
> to destroy the temple of God and to build it in three
> days.'" The high priest stood up and said, "Have you
> no answer? What is it that they testify against you?"
> (Matthew 26:59-62, NRSV).

The whole trial centers on the question of identity. Does Jesus claim to be the Messiah? It's a reasonable question to ask a man who rode into Jerusalem on a donkey to fulfill a well-known messianic prophecy:

> But Jesus was silent. Then the high priest said to him,
> "I put you under oath before the living God, tell us if
> you are the Messiah, the Son of God" (Matthew
> 26:63, NRSV).

The Son of Man Will Judge the Judges

Jesus doesn't answer this question, but he responds even more provocatively with his statement about the Son of Man. The Son of Man is the one who will judge the rulers when God institutes the kingdom of heaven on Earth.

Here he is claiming the identity of the Son of Man who will come to judge the high priest and all of the ruling priests, elders, and leaders of Israel:

> Jesus said to him, "You have said so. But I tell you,
> From now on you will see the Son of Man seated at

the right hand of Power and coming on the clouds of heaven" (Matthew 26:64, NRSV).

Guilty of Blasphemy

This is enough for the high priest to declare that Jesus is guilty of blasphemy, a capital offense. Blasphemy refers to slander, cursing, or showing contempt for God. One way to commit blasphemy is to claim that you have the authority of God to judge the religious and civic leaders of Israel:

> Then the high priest tore his clothes and said, "He has blasphemed! Why do we still need witnesses? You have now heard his blasphemy. What is your verdict?" They answered, "He deserves death." Then they spat in his face and struck him; and some slapped him, saying, "Prophesy to us, you Messiah! Who is it that struck you?" (Matthew 26:65-68, NRSV).

The entire trial focuses on what Jesus has claimed about his own identity. First, his very public ride into Jerusalem demonstrated his claim that he is the Messiah who is coming to take possession of kingly rule. Second, he makes the obvious claim that he is the Son of Man who will judge the hierarchy and the rulers. Jesus is not innocent in any of this.

Are You King of the Jews?

Since the religious leaders do not have the legal authority to execute Jesus, they send him to the Roman governor, Pontius Pilate:

> Now Jesus stood before the governor; and the governor asked him, "Are you the King of the Jews?" Jesus said, "You say so" (Matthew 27:11, NRSV).

Once again, the question concerns the identity of Jesus. Pilate asks Jesus if he is King of the Jews. It is actually the same question as the one asked by Caiaphas. The expected Messiah is to become the King of the Jews.

The story then goes to great lengths to exonerate Pilate from the decision to execute Jesus, by having the chief priests and elders persuade the crowds to demand that Jesus be executed. When Pilate asks the crowds about Jesus, he uses the terminology of Messiah:

> Pilate said to them, "Then what should I do with Jesus who is called the Messiah?" All of them said, "Let him be crucified!" (Matthew 27:22, NRSV).

Death and Resurrection

In the hero's journey, the hero encounters death a second time. This is the *climax* of the story. The hero faces death in a final confrontation with the ultimate adversary. In most stories, the hero cheats death. In some stories, the hero dies at this point. But all have some sort of *resurrection* experience, in which the hero survives death or, in some way, lives on in memory.

The narrative about the crucifixion also makes clear that Jesus is being executed because of his claim to be the Messiah, the King of the Jews.

First, the Roman soldiers dress him in mock king's robe, crown, and scepter, and kneel before him in mock obedience to the King of the Jews:

> Then the soldiers of the governor took Jesus into the governor's headquarters, and they gathered the whole cohort around him. They stripped him and put a scarlet robe on him, and after twisting some thorns into a crown, they put it on his head. They put a reed in his right hand and knelt before him and mocked him, saying, "Hail, King of the Jews!" They spat on

> him, and took the reed and struck him on the head. After mocking him, they stripped him of the robe and put his own clothes on him. Then they led him away to crucify him (Matthew 27:27-31, NRSV).

The charge against him is posted on the cross itself. He is guilty of the blasphemous claim that he is the Messiah, the King of the Jews:

> And when they had crucified him, they divided his clothes among themselves by casting lots; then they sat down there and kept watch over him. Over his head they put the charge against him, which read, "This is Jesus, the King of the Jews" (Matthew 27:35-37, NRSV).

While he hangs on the cross, everyone who sees him mocks him about his identity claims as the Messiah and the Son of God:

> Then two bandits were crucified with him, one on his right and one on his left. Those who passed by derided him, shaking their heads and saying, "You who would destroy the temple and build it in three days, save yourself! If you are the Son of God, come down from the cross." In the same way the chief priests also, along with the scribes and elders, were mocking him, saying, "He saved others; he cannot save himself. He is the King of Israel; let him come down from the cross now, and we will believe in him. He trusts in God; let God deliver him now, if he wants to; for he said, 'I am God's Son.'" The bandits who were crucified with him also taunted him in the same way. (Matthew 27:38-44, NRSV).

And to make the whole arc of his hero's journey complete, even the bandits who are being executed with him taunt him in the words used by the devil in the wilderness: "If you are the Son of God, come down from the cross."

It's all here. The temptation that Jesus withstood in the wilderness. His identity as the Messiah. His identity as the Son of God. His identity as a hero.

Why Have You Abandoned Me?

Although Good Friday services about the "seven last words of Christ" gather the words of Jesus from the cross from all four gospels, in Matthew, Jesus has only one statement, in Aramaic:

> And about three o'clock Jesus cried with a loud voice, "Eli, Eli, lema sabachthani?" that is, "My God, my God, why have you forsaken me?" (Matthew 27:46, NRSV).

In the context of Matthew's Gospel, these words are especially poignant. Twice in the story, Jesus heard words from above: "This is my Son, the Beloved, with whom I am well pleased."

But here, after traveling on the journey to fulfill his identity as the Messiah—the Son of God—God is silent. This time there is no voice from above. This time, Jesus doesn't hear the words that he is "the Beloved." This time, he does not call God "Father."

At this point, this looks like a failed hero's journey. The savior cannot save anyone, least of all himself. The hero did not accomplish his mission, and God abandoned him.

Returning to the Ordinary World

After the sabbath, the two Marys go to the tomb:

> After the sabbath, as the first day of the week was dawning, Mary Magdalene and the other Mary went to see the tomb. And suddenly there was a great earthquake; for an angel of the Lord, descending from heaven, came and rolled back the stone and sat

on it. His appearance was like lightning, and his clothing white as snow. For fear of him the guards shook and became like dead men (Matthew 28:1-4, NRSV).

The particular detail to comment on here is the appearance of the angel. It recalls the experience of the Transfiguration, when Jesus' face "shone like the sun, and his clothes became dazzling white" (17:2). Here the appearance of the angel "was like lightning, and his clothing white as snow."

Both of these encounters are evidence of connection with the spiritual world.

Back to Galilee

Then the angel gives the two Marys a message:

> But the angel said to the women, "Do not be afraid; I know that you are looking for Jesus who was crucified. He is not here; for he has been raised, as he said. Come, see the place where he lay. Then go quickly and tell his disciples, 'He has been raised from the dead, and indeed he is going ahead of you to Galilee; there you will see him.' This is my message for you" (Matthew 28:5-7, NRSV).

Then the women meet Jesus himself and he gives the same message:

> So they left the tomb quickly with fear and great joy, and ran to tell his disciples. Suddenly Jesus met them and said, "Greetings!" And they came to him, took hold of his feet, and worshiped him. Then Jesus said to them, "Do not be afraid; go and tell my brothers to go to Galilee; there they will see me" (Matthew 28: 8-10, NRSV).

The message is for the disciples to return to Galilee. For the journey to be complete, the hero goes home again, back to his ordinary world. This means going back to Galilee, where the journey started.

Return with the Elixir

The essential idea of a hero's journey is that the hero is going on the journey for the benefit of others. Something is wrong in the hero's ordinary world. The hero sets out to confront the threat, solve the problem, and restore balance to the ordinary world. For the hero's journey to be complete, the hero returns home, bringing some healing gift.

Campbell called the healing gift the *elixir*. The word comes from Arabic and can refer to the philosopher's stone of the alchemists, which had the capacity to turn base metals into gold. It can be a potion with magical healing and life-extending power. It can be love. It can be the capacity find a balance between the spiritual and material worlds. Whatever it is, the elixir is the reason the hero set out on the journey. The hero must bring the elixir home to make the journey complete:

> Now the eleven disciples went to Galilee, to the mountain to which Jesus had directed them. When they saw him, they worshiped him; but some doubted. And Jesus came and said to them, "All authority in heaven and on earth has been given to me. Go therefore and make disciples of all nations, baptizing them in the name of the Father and of the Son and of the Holy Spirit, and teaching them to obey everything that I have commanded you. And remember, I am with you always, to the end of the age" (Matthew 28:16-20, NRSV).

These final words are the final claim of his identity. In Campbell's terminology, Jesus is the Master of Two Worlds.

In the language of the kingdom of heaven, he has become the promised Messiah, with all authority on heaven and earth. This authority includes commanding his disciples to make more disciples in the name of the Father, Son, and Holy Spirit.

But what is the elixir that the resurrected Jesus brings back to Galilee? It is the elixir of presence: "And remember, I am with you always, to the end of the age."

Part Seven

Identities

of

Those Who Trap Little Ones

Chapter 22
The Identity of the Greatest
In the Kingdom

> Everywhere, everywhere, children are
> the scorned people of the earth.
>
> Toni Morrison

Who Is Greatest in the Kingdom of Heaven?

It's now time to go back to Chapter 18 of the Gospel of Matthew. We started with the first phrase of 18:6, which is a grammatically simple Greek phrase with the clear sense of "if anyone traps one of the little ones..." The overwhelming tendency of English language Bible translators is to complicate the phrase grammatically by assigning particular actions to the little ones, so that they stumble or trip or fall into sin.

Even if a translation doesn't explicitly use the word "sin," the sense is clear. Sin juice turns traps into stumbling blocks, which effectively deflects the focus from the ones who trap to the ones who "trip."

There is no instance in the Gospel of Matthew where Jesus identifies the little ones as sinners. However, it is manifestly clear that Jesus condemns with ferocity the actions of the religious establishment to shut the little ones out of the kingdom of heaven.

The trap language of Matthew 18:6 is consistent with the biblical language of the authority to block, shut, close, and lock *access to the holy*. To imply that the little ones are sinners because the religious establishment blocks their way, shuts them out, closes the gates, and locks the doors is a profoundly distorted sense of the entire Gospel of Matthew.

Chapter 18 comes after the long Road of Trials, in which Jesus has proclaimed that the kingdom of heaven is near. It comes after the transformative event of the ordeal—the transfiguration—when Jesus experiences his divinity in a radiant display before three of his disciples. It comes after Jesus tells his disciples that he is going to Jerusalem to die and to be resurrected on the third day.

After all of this, what do his disciples want to know?:

> At that time the disciples came to Jesus and asked, "Who is the greatest in the kingdom of heaven?" (Matthew 18:1, NRSV).

The Child as Object Lesson

Jesus responds to this question with a demonstration:

> He called a child, whom he put among them, and said, "Truly I tell you, unless you change and become like children, you will never enter the kingdom of heaven. Whoever becomes humble like this child is the greatest in the kingdom of heaven. Whoever welcomes one such child in my name welcomes me. (Matthew 18:2-5, NRSV).

This answer is the parabolic spoon that Jesus holds up before the disciples. It conveys the essence of what he means by entering the kingdom of heaven, not only here, but throughout the Gospel of Matthew. If you see the image here, you see it everywhere.

But too often, we don't see the image in the spoon, because the parabola has turned into a flat surface, the parables have turned into mortality tales, and we have missed the point.

The most critical insight for reading all of Chapter 18 is to recognize that Jesus uses the child as an *object lesson*. Jesus says nothing here about the "sins" of the little ones. However, he does refer to their faith. All he says about the little ones is that they "believe in me."

None of what follows in Chapter 18 is about what children or little ones must do to enter the kingdom of heaven. Instead, every word is directed to the ones who have the power to block the "humble" from entering the kingdom of heaven.

Entering the Kingdom of Heaven

The single greatest misunderstanding of contemporary Bible readers about the kingdom of heaven language in the Gospel of Matthew is the difference between *getting into heaven* and *entering into the kingdom of heaven*. It begins with confusion over "heaven" and the "kingdom of heaven." The kingdom of heaven is about life on earth, not an afterlife in heaven.

This means that the critical action is not *getting into* but *entering into*. "Getting into" is the language of passing admission requirements, the way you "get into a college" or "get into a club" or "get into a job." Someone else judges if you meet the qualifications. But Jesus doesn't use the language of "getting into" the kingdom. Instead, he uses the language of *entering into*. This is the language of choice.

If you read the Gospel of Matthew closely, you will see that being a disciple of Jesus requires giving up all privileges, status, wealth, and power. When he calls his disciples, he tells them to leave everything and follow him. This is why the elite, the rich, and the powerful *will not enter* under those terms.

It is also the reason why the ones who follow Jesus are the little ones, not the powerful ones. They are the poor, the beggars, the outcasts, the sick. They are excluded from wealth and power by economic injustices in a world of social and economic stratification. They are also excluded by religion, because of a complicated system of rules about cleanness and holiness, which excludes most people.

This is why the words of Jesus are so tough. In a world shaped by social stratification and religious categories, Jesus says that those who enter into the kingdom of heaven must choose to enter by giving up their status and their privileges.

This is also why is it much easier for contemporary Christians to see what Jesus says as rules for "getting into" a heavenly afterlife than words about social, economic, and religious injustices in this life. It's so much more comfortable to see what Jesus says as statements about the salvation of "sinful" little ones, than to see that Jesus is condemning those who exclude the little ones from the blessings of God.

This is also why it is so much more comfortable to read Chapter 18 as a diagnosis of why "little ones fall into sin" rather than to see the full force of the condemnation of Jesus toward the ones who trap, block, and lead astray the little ones who would willingly enter the kingdom if they were not trapped, blocked, and led astray.

What Does "Humble" Mean?

The NRSV translation uses the word "humble." What does this word mean here? English has several connotations:

- One has to do with your own sense of yourself. You are *humble* if you are modest, self-effacing, and meek, rather than proud, arrogant, and egotistical. You can also feel humble in comparison with others who are "greater" than you in some way. In comparison, you feel insignificant and inferior.

- Humble also has the connotation of being shamed, humiliated, and brought down in your own estimation of yourself and what others think about you.

- Humble can also refer to status and rank. You come from "humble" origins, and live in a "humble" home.

In sin-soaked churches, where "pride" is the sin that must be repented above all others, the connotation most favored by preachers and Bible teachers concerns your inflated sense of yourself. You must lower your estimation of yourself.

Only the Low Will Enter the Kingdom of Heaven

But to treat "humble" as simply a matter of your own sense of self-importance is to miss the essence of Matthew's Gospel. This kind of humility is not the meaning here in Matthew. The verb is *tapeinóō*.

Although the Greek word has a similar range of meanings as English, it begins with the idea of *being low*. You are "humble" because of your lack of status. A child is "humble" because a child has no power, no wealth, no status, no rank.

A better sense of what Jesus intends here would be, "Whoever becomes as low [in status] as this child is the greatest in the kingdom of heaven."

In effect, Jesus says: "Who is greatest in the kingdom of heaven?" is the wrong question. The kingdom of the world is defined by such questions. The kingdom of the world is defined by status and power and wealth and rank. In contrast, the ones who are greatest in the kingdom of heaven have no power, no wealth, no status, and no rank.

Unless You Turn

NRSV translates "unless you change and become like children, you will never enter the kingdom of heaven." The key word here is the verb. (In my experience, the most significant insights almost always concern the meaning of the verb.)

The verb is *strépho*, which means, *to turn*. It's not a matter of changing something within yourself, it's a matter of *turning away* from wealth and status, to become powerless, to become one of the lowest of the low.

Consider how the CEB translates the verb:

> Then he called a little child over to sit among the disciples, and said, "I assure you that if you don't turn your lives around and become like the little child, you will definitely not enter the kingdom of heaven. Those who humble themselves like this child will be the greatest in the kingdom of heaven. Whoever welcomes one such child in my name welcomes me (Matthew 18:2-5, CEB).

Once again, the CEB has made it personal and added an explanatory gloss. The verb *strépho* means *turn*. The words, "your life around" are an addition to the Greek, which focuses on "you." The idea of "turn your lives around" sounds like a personal makeover, when you "turn your life around" from failure, or loss, or addiction, or some destructive behavior. It doesn't convey the sense that entering the kingdom of heaven means a willingness to turn away from your own sense of status and superiority and advantage.

The parabolic vision in the spoon that Jesus holds up to his disciples concerns the willingness to turn away from any sense that they deserve God's blessing, but the little ones don't.

To read any part of the Gospel of Matthew, without setting it into the Whole Story context of the social, economic, and religious injustices of first century Palestine is to miss the essence of the story. For Jesus, it was a society divided between the haves and have–nots, the included and the excluded, the elite and the little ones, built on a religious system that violated the sense of Torah.

It's the same parabolic vision that the Gospel of Matthew holds up to any Christian church when it separates the "worthy" from the "unworthy" because of social   status, wealth, rank, age, gender, race, or sexuality—or any other distinction—in a way that elevates "the worthy" while debasing others.

This meaning of *turn* gets to the heart of what religious groups tend to do, when they decide that they have the right to block access to God by others they judge unworthy.

Chapter 23
Identities
of
Those Who Lock the Kingdom

Injustice is relatively easy to bear; what
stings is justice.

Henry Louis Mencken

Woe to You

Matthew 18:6-10 is what biblical scholars call a *woe oracle*. Woe means pain, discomfort, and unhappiness. The phrase, "woe is me," is often used for comic relief. It's even the name of a rock band. But there is nothing funny about the biblical meaning of *woe*. The language of woe is the language of judgment. It is the opposite of the language of *blessing*. Words of woe intend the worst for someone. Words of blessing intend the best.

The Hebrew prophets used a characteristic formula to pronounce judgment against a person or group of persons. The woe oracle is an intense denunciation and reproach, which includes name-calling and a threat, followed by more detail.

However, both the NRSV and the CEB have obscured the woe oracle by their paragraphing and translation decisions. To get the full impact of a woe oracle, let's look first at Matthew 23.

Pronouncing Woe against the Scribes and Pharisees

In Matthew 23, Jesus pronounces seven woes against the scribes and Pharisees.

Before pronouncing his seven woes against them, Jesus begins by making claims about the scribes and Pharisees:

> Then Jesus said to the crowds and to his disciples, "The scribes and the Pharisees sit on Moses' seat; therefore, do whatever they teach you and follow it; but do not do as they do, for they do not practice what they teach.
>
> They tie up heavy burdens, hard to bear, and lay them on the shoulders of others; but they themselves are unwilling to lift a finger to move them.
>
> They do all their deeds to be seen by others; for they make their phylacteries broad and their fringes long.
>
> They love to have the place of honor at banquets and the best seats in the synagogues, and to be greeted with respect in the marketplaces, and to have people call them rabbi.
>
> But you are not to be called rabbi, for you have one teacher, and you are all students. And call no one your father on earth, for you have one Father—the one in heaven. Nor are you to be called instructors, for you have one instructor, the Messiah.
>
> The greatest among you will be your servant. All who exalt themselves will be humbled, and all who humble themselves will be exalted (Matthew 23:1-12, NRSV).

Then he pronounces seven woes upon them. This is the first one:

> But woe to you, scribes and Pharisees, hypocrites!
> For you lock people out of the Kingdom of heaven.
> For you do not go in yourselves, and when others are
> going in, you stop them (Matthew 23:13, NRSV).

The Ones Who Lock the Kingdom

This first woe can serve as the hologram for the whole of Matthew's Gospel. The mission of Jesus is to invite people to enter into the kingdom of heaven. Throughout his journey, the scribes and Pharisees dog his footsteps, challenge his authority, and plot to destroy him.

Jesus says that the scribes and Pharisees "lock people out of the kingdom of heaven." The verb is *kleiō*. It means to shut, to close, to block, to lock. This language of closing and locking is familiar biblical language for the authority to either allow or block access to what is *holy*.

One example occurs in Isaiah:

> On that day I will call my servant Eliakim son of
> Hilkiah, and will clothe him with your robe and bind
> your sash on him. I will commit your authority to his
> hand, and he shall be a father to the inhabitants of
> Jerusalem and to the house of Judah. I will place on
> his shoulder the key of the house of David; he shall
> open, and no one shall shut; he shall shut, and no
> one shall open (Isaiah 22:20-22, NRSV).

The Keys of the Kingdom

Jesus draws on these biblical images of the authority to open and close when he asks his disciples about his identity in Caesarea Philippi:

> He said to them, "But who do you say that I am?"
> Simon Peter answered, "You are the Messiah, the
> Son of the living God" (Matthew 16:15-16, NRSV).

In response to this answer, Jesus tells Peter that he will give him the keys of the kingdom of heaven:

> And Jesus answered him, "Blessed are you, Simon son of Jonah! For flesh and blood has not revealed this to you, but my Father in heaven.
>
> And I tell you, you are Peter, and on this rock I will build my church, and the gates of Hades will not prevail against it.
>
> I will give you the keys of the kingdom of heaven, and whatever you bind on earth will be bound in heaven, and whatever you loose on earth will be loosed in heaven" (Matthew 16:17-19, NRSV).

These particular verses are the basis for the claim of the Roman Catholic Church that the Pope has supreme authority over the entire Christian church. The papal keys are the foundational symbol of his authority.

Jesus says that the scribes and Pharisees lock people out of the kingdom of heaven but they don't have the authority to do it. Peter, as the "rock" on which the church is built, has the authority because he acknowledges Jesus as "the Messiah, the Son of the living God." This is what the scribes and Pharisees will not do.

This is why the first woe in Chapter 23 is to the scribes and Pharisees, because they lock out the ones who want to enter the kingdom of heaven, but they themselves will not enter.

Chapter 24
Hiding the Identities
Of the Culprits

The guilty are all too anxious to lay
blame on the innocent.

Arthur Tugman

Woe to the World

Matthew 18:6-9 is another woe oracle, with the same
pattern as the seven woe oracles of Chapter 23. As a woe
oracle, it is unusual because it doesn't name a specific
person or group of persons, such as the scribes or Pharisees.
Instead, it is a woe oracle addressed to "anyone" who does a
specific action against "one of the little ones who believe in
me."

"If anyone traps one of these little ones who believe in
me..." is followed by a harsh statement about what such a
person deserves. That person deserves to be drowned with
a rock around the neck.

After this statement of the charge and the appropriate
response to such wrongdoing, this is the NRSV translation
of what Jesus says in this woe oracle:

> Woe to the world because of stumbling blocks!
> Occasions for stumbling are bound to come, but woe
> to the one by whom the stumbling block comes!
> (Matthew 18:7, NRSV).

The CEB translates the same verse this way:

> How terrible it is for the world because of the things that cause people to trip and fall into sin! Such things have to happen, but how terrible it is for the person who causes those things to happen (Matthew 18:7, CEB).

The "world" is *kósmos*. It has a wide range of meanings, just as *world* does in English:

- It can be the universe—the cosmos—as the sum total of all that exists.

- It can be the world, as planet earth.

- It can be the earth in contrast to heaven.

- It can be all human inhabitants of the earth.

- It can be the world beyond home.

- It can mean the world as a way of life.

Although 18:6 is straightforward Greek, 18:7 is not so clear. After considerable research into the grammar and word meanings, I come to these two conclusions: The first is that I am not certain that I understand the Greek here. The second is that I am quite certain that neither the NRSV nor the CEB do either.

Is This Practical Atheism?

The source of the problem is the Greek word *anánkē*. In Greek culture, *anánkē* was the power that determined all reality. It is fate. It is necessity, obligation, compulsion. However, neither a Hebraic nor a New Testament Christian worldview attributes anything that happens in the world to "fate." All that happens is under the control of God's will, including God's willingness to allow human beings free will to act contrary to God's will.

Alistair McFadyen's book, *Bound To Sin: Abuse, Holocaust, and the Christian Doctrine of Sin*, is a careful study of the doctrine of sin by a Christian theologian. His book includes his claim that even the idea of "sin" is largely *irrelevant* in our era. McFadyen defines sin as "disruption of our proper relation to God" (McFadyen 5).

I cite McFadyen here, not to argue for or against his theological claims, but to use his definition of sin for a fresh perspective on the Gospel of Matthew. In the Gospel of Matthew, Jesus makes clear that the ones who disrupt "proper relation to God" are not the little ones, but the ones who trap the little ones.

The premise McFadyen intends to argue in his book is this:

> If God is the most basic reality and explanation of the world, then it must be the case that the world cannot *adequately* [emphasis in the original] be explained, understood, lived in, without reference to God in our fundamental means both of discernment and of action (McFadyen 12).

He then makes this provocative statement:

> Hence, we live in a culture that shapes us all, in our most basic ways of making sense of and intending ourselves and our world as practical atheists (McFadyen 9).

When I read how NRSV and CEB translate this phrase, I think of this statement about "practical atheism." The translations, "occasions for stumbling are bound to come" and "such things have to happen," strike me as inconsistent with a *theistic* worldview, in which there is no such thing as "fate." Both translations convey the sense of, "bad stuff happens," with no reference to God's role.

Translating an Idiom

In addition, the noun *anánkē* was used idiomatically in Greek culture with the sense of a verb, to indicate something you are *compelled* to do.

An idiom is a peculiar use of words that make no sense if you take them literally. Idiomatic expressions are one reason why learning another language is often so difficult. Native speakers in a region use strange statements that baffle non-native speakers. For example, if someone says that it's raining cats and dogs, do you really expect to see a sky-full of wet tabby cats and golden retrievers falling to the ground?

The Bible has its share of idiomatic expressions in its original languages that baffle contemporary translators, including this idiomatic use of *anánkē*.

It seems that the construction here has to do with an idiomatic usage of a noun to function as a verb, which relates to an inevitable inner or outer compulsion to do something that you or someone else must do.

The same word occurs elsewhere in the New Testament, where it is no easier to translate. It all depends on whether you think *anánkē* refers to:

- inner or outer compulsion

- that the world is ruled by impersonal fate or by God's will

- whether you are the one doing the compelling or the one being compelled

My tentative sense of the meaning here is that *anánkē* refers to the use of power to compel others in some way.

The NRSV translation, with its vague, "occasions for stumbling may come," and the CEB with its equally vague, "such things have to happen," take the focus away from the ones who trap. Then it becomes a statement of how the little ones are going to stumble from time to time, because that is just the way life is, here on planet earth. And once again, the CEB gratuitously introduces sin language into a passage where sin is not mentioned:

> How terrible it is for the world because of the things that cause people to trip and fall into sin!   Such things have to happen, but how terrible it is for the person who causes those things to happen (Matthew 18:7, CEB).

Woe to the Ones Who Trap

However, when this phrase is recognized for what it is—a part of a woe oracle that Jesus pronounces against the ones who trap the little ones—then this phrase doesn't refer to fate, or God's will, or just the way things are. It becomes a condemnation of what those with power do to compel the little ones into traps.

Although I don't claim that this is an accurate translation of the Greek here, I suspect that the sense of 18:7 is something like this:

> Woe comes to the world because of traps. [People] are forced into traps. But woe to the one who sets the traps.

After this statement of the charge of wrongdoing, Jesus then has more harsh words for the ones who trap. Once again, look at how the NRSV translates the verses, with "stumble" language:

> If your hand or your foot causes you to stumble, cut it off and throw it away; it is better for you to enter life maimed or lame than to have two hands or two feet and to be thrown into the eternal fire. And if your eye causes you to stumble, tear it out and throw it away; it is better for you to enter life with

> one eye than to have two eyes and to be thrown
> into the hell of fire (Matthew 18:8-9, NRSV).

Once again, the "stumble" language diverts attention from the trappers to the ones who are trapped. If the little ones are the ones who "stumble over stumbling blocks," then these words seem to apply to the little ones.

But the Greek doesn't say this. This is a woe oracle addressed to the one who traps. It's clear if the "cause to stumble" language becomes "set a trap" language.

With these minimal revisions, marked in italics, the NRSV translation becomes:

> If your hand or your foot causes you to *set a trap*, cut it off and throw it away; it is better for you to enter life maimed or lame than to have two hands or two feet and to be thrown into the eternal fire. And if your eye causes you to *set a trap*, tear it out and throw it away; it is better for you to enter life with one eye than to have two eyes and to be thrown into the hell of fire (Matthew 18:8-9, NRSV, revised by KRS).

To Enter Life

One more significant item here deserves notice. It is the phrase translated as, "to enter life."

Herman Waetjen asserts that when Jesus refers to *eternal life*, he is not referring to life after death. Instead, the phrase refers to life under the rule of God. It's not about getting into heaven after you die, but about life in the kingdom of God. Significantly, the way to gain eternal life is by practicing justice. As Waetjen puts it:

> "Eternal life" is gained by the fulfillment of justice in human relationships... (Waetjen 169).

This reading is consistent with the mission of Jesus in the Gospel of Matthew. He invites people to enter into the kingdom of God on earth—the rule of God—a rule that is not based on status, rank, power, privilege, and wealth.

Do Not Look Down on the Little Ones

This woe oracle ends with yet another reminder that those who enter the kingdom of heaven must be "humble" by giving away their privilege:

> Take care that you do not despise one of these little ones; for, I tell you, in heaven their angels continually see the face of my Father in heaven (Matthew 18:10, NRSV).

The significant word here is "despise." Once again, the NRSV word choice doesn't quite convey the sense of the meaning. The word is *kataphronéō*. It is not about hating someone, but about *looking down on* someone who is of lower status—the poor and the outcast.

In Jesus' vision of the Kingdom of heaven, the little ones—the ones who are without power, wealth, or status in the kingdom of the world—are the ones who enter the kingdom of heaven. It is a vision of social justice, and it is consistent with the whole of Matthew's Gospel.

All of this means that Matthew 18:6-10 is a woe oracle addressed to anyone who uses power, privilege, and wealth to trap the powerless, the excluded ones, the impoverished ones. None of it is addressed to "little ones who stumble into sin." All of it—every word of it—is addressed to those who block the little ones from entering into the kingdom of heaven.

A Sin-Soaked Translation

As one more example of how sin-soaked translations make it all be about "you" as the sinner, I include the CEB translation of these verses:

> As for whoever cause these little ones who believe in me to trip and fall into sin, it would be better for them to have a huge stone hung around their necks and be drowned in the bottom of the lake.

> How terrible it is for the world because of the things that cause people to trip and fall into sin! Such things have to happen, but how terrible it is for the person who causes those things to happen. If your hand or your foot causes you to fall into sin, chop it off and throw it away. it's better to enter into life crippled or lame than to be thrown in the eternal fire with two hands or two feet. If your eye causes you to fall into sin, tear it out and throw it away. it's better to enter into life with one eye than to be cast into a burning hell with two eyes (Matthew 18:6-9).

The CEB then disconnects the final verse of the woe oracle, and treats it as the beginning of the next parable.

> Be careful that you don't look down upon one of these little ones. For I say to you that their angels in heaven are always looking in the face of my Father who is in heaven (Matthew 18:10).

What Happened to the Judgment against Wrongdoers?

This translation completely loses all sense of a woe oracle, both because it doesn't use the word woe and because it splits off the last part of the oracle. I suspect it is one more case where the CEB's intention to turn "archaic" language into familiar English replaces the strong woe language of the Hebrew prophets as judgments against wrongdoers into the familiar language of "how terrible" that bad things happen.

A woe oracle is directed against a wrongdoer. This vague statement about "how terrible it is," with no sense that anyone is responsible, is not a woe oracle. It really does demonstrate practical atheism. Bad stuff happens. This might in fact be the reality of our world, but it is not a theistic, biblical worldview.

This translation also loses the sense that the whole woe oracle is addressed to someone who is being judged harshly for actions done to the vulnerable little ones. And the inexcusable substitution of "people" for "little ones"—"How terrible it is for the world because of the things that cause *people* to trip and fall into sin!"—makes it all generic, rather than specifically focused on the vulnerable "little ones" of the Gospel of Matthew. The vision of social justice for the little ones in the Gospel of Matthew is replaced by a sin-soaked translation about how "you fall into sin."

The doctrine of original sin and the salvation theology of the Christian church have obscured how much the Gospel of Matthew is about saving the little ones from injustice. The CEB translation reinforces American individualism, with the idea that Jesus is your personal savior. To turn this story into personal salvation doctrine is to completely miss the worldview of Jesus in Matthew.

In the process, it misses the emphasis on social justice for the little ones—the outcasts, the expendables, the ones with no social status, no wealth, and no power. And it misses the harsh condemnation of Jesus against anyone who treats little ones unjustly.

As a woe oracle, Matthew 18:6-11 has the same intention as the woe oracle Jesus addressed to the scribes and Pharisees in Matthew 23:

> "But woe to you, scribes and Pharisees, hypocrites!
> For you lock people out of the Kingdom of heaven.
> For you do not go in yourselves, and when others are
> going in, you stop them (Matthew 23:13, NRSV).

The Woe Oracle of Matthew 18:6-10

Here is the whole of Matthew 18:6-10, with minimal revisions to the NRSV. My goal here is to give a sense of the whole as a woe oracle addressed to a wrongdoer, without claiming that it is the best possible translation. My substitutions are in italics:

> If any of you *traps* one of these little ones who believe in me, it would be better for you if a great millstone were fastened around your neck and you were drowned in the depth of the sea. Woe [comes] to the world because of *traps*! [Little ones] are *compelled into traps*, but woe to the one *who sets the traps!*
>
> If your hand or your foot causes you to *set traps*, cut it off and throw it away; it is better for you to enter life maimed or lame than to have two hands or two feet and to be thrown into the eternal fire. And if your eye causes you to *set traps*, tear it out and throw it away; it is better for you to enter life with one eye than to have two eyes and to be thrown into the hell of fire.
>
> Take care that you do not *look down on* one of these little ones; for, I tell you, in heaven their angels continually see the face of my Father in heaven (Matthew 18:6-10, NRSV, revised KRS).

All of this began with the question of the disciples about who was greatest in the kingdom of heaven. Jesus used a child as an object lesson to make the point that the question itself completely misses the essence of the kingdom of heaven.

The essential point is that *no one is greatest* in the kingdom of heaven. There is no division based on status, no contempt for those beneath you, no treating the ones without power—the children, the poor, the degraded, the expendables—as unworthy.

Chapter 25
What Is the True Identity
Of the Lost Sheep?

I swore never to be silent whenever and wherever human beings endure suffering and humiliation. We must always take sides. Neutrality helps the oppressor, never the victim. Silence encourages the tormentor, never the tormented.

Elie Wiesel

Blaming the Sheep

Very briefly, what comes next in Chapter 18 is the story about the lost sheep, which is consistent with everything that has come before in the chapter. It's not about what the sheep do, it's about what's done to the sheep.

Here's the NRSV translation. Notice what the verb choice claims about the sheep. This is another conditional sentence, beginning with a dependent clause. *If this happens, then this will be the result*:

What do you think? If a shepherd has a hundred sheep, and one of them has gone astray, does he not leave the ninety-nine on the mountains and go in search of the one that went astray? And if he finds it, truly I tell you, he rejoices over it more than over the ninety-nine that never went astray. So it is not the

> will of your Father in heaven that one of these little
> ones should be lost (Matthew 18:12-14, NRSV).

I'll point out only one detail here. Once again, the NRSV translation has transferred blame to the little ones by mistranslating the verb.

The root verb is *planáō*. As an active verb, it means *to lead astray, to mislead, to deceive*. As a passive verb, it means *to be led astray, to be misled, to be deceived*.

Here, the verbal form is a passive participle in the accusative case. The accusative case is used for the direct object of the action identified by the verb. The direct object doesn't do the action of the verb. It is the *passive recipient* of the action done by another. In this case, the sheep was *led astray* by the actions of another. It did not *go astray*.

But the NRSV translation doesn't say: "If a shepherd has a hundred sheep, and one of them is led astray..." Instead, it blames the sheep, by translating "one of them has gone astray."

What the NRSV has done here is similar to the translations of Matthew 18:6, in which the direct object becomes the actor rather than the recipient of the action. We are once again back to the difference between "Fred kicked the cat" and "Fred caused the cat to jump up and scratch him."

The CEB makes it even more explicit:

> If someone had a hundred sheep, and one of them
> wandered off..." (Matthew 18: 12, CEB).

If you look at English translations, you will see the same tendency to refer to wandering sheep and the ones who go astray. You will be far less likely to read about sheep that are led astray, misled, deceived.

Diverting Attention

Three times in Chapter 18, the overwhelming tendency of translations is to divert attention from the one with power to the one without power, to reinforce the idea that "you" are a sinner who needs to be saved.

- It begins with the translation of "humble" without making clear that the meaning here is not about a prideful sense of self-importance but about social status.

- It continues with the "stumbling block" language, which turns the little ones into sinners, while missing the real point that this is a woe oracle against those who trap the little ones.

- And finally, it turns the ones who are *led off* into ones who *wander off*.

The idea that people are errant sinners—lost sheep who need to be saved—is so deeply embedded in Christian consciousness that the true force of the condemnation of Jesus turns into a series of stories about little ones who become sinners because they "stumble," "fall into sin," or "wander" off.

In Christian tradition, clergy are often called "pastors." The word *pastor* itself is derived from the Latin word for *shepherd*. The role of the pastor as shepherd is so deeply rooted in Christian vocabulary that "pastors" are responsible for tending to their "flocks." Then the words of Jesus in Matthew 18 become guidance for "the shepherds" to round up the errant sheep and bring them back into the fold.

These translations, with their overwhelming tendency to call little ones sinners, obscures the real target of the condemnation of Jesus intends by the woe oracle. He condemns the religious leaders for blocking the little ones from entering the kingdom.

A Personal Story

I will end this section about Matthew 18 with another personal story.

Earlier, I told you about my visit to the minister of my home church, to ask if he would serve as an intermediary so that I could do something to change my relationship with my parents.

In the spring of my sophomore year, I began to talk with the minister of the Congregational Church I attended during most of my first three years at the university. I will call him Mr. Brown. Once again, my focus was on what to do about my relationship with my parents. We talked quite regularly over parts of my sophomore and junior years.

Starting from the time I began Sunday School at the age of three, my entire Christian education could be summarized in three imperatives:

- Honor your parents by obeying everything they tell you to do.

- Obey authority.

- Give away the best of everything you have to other people.

Honor Your Parents, No Matter What

The really tough one was the one about honoring my parents. I grew up terrified of the Father God in Heaven who was on the side of my parents, the one who would punish me if I ever, ever told the secrets of what went on at home.

Honor your father and your mother is another Bible verse that has been turned upside down. Now, after significant study of the Ten Commandments in Hebrew, I am certain that the commandment to honor your father and your mother in Exodus 20:12 is not about the obedience of children to their parents. It is about the responsibly of the head of the household to take care of his elderly parents.

However, instead of making clear that the Hebrew is referring to the obligation of the ones with power to take care of the vulnerable, much Christian teaching misuses this commandment to demand the obedience of the vulnerable to the powerful.

This interpretation ignores the significant fact that the word in Hebrew means *honor,* which doesn't mean the same as *obey*, either in Hebrew or in English.

But I didn't know any of this as a terrified and vulnerable child in Sunday School.

Even as a very young child, I knew that my parents were abusive and neglectful. When I saw the picture in my reading book in the second grade, I decided that I would leave that house as soon as I was old enough and never go back. It became my only enduring hope for the future.

I escaped when I went off to the university, but it wasn't as easy to escape a lifetime of Christian commands to obey the people who had tormented me.

With hindsight, I realize that Mr. Brown had no more capacity to help me than the clueless Mr. Edwards. Mr. Brown told me that I "shouldn't" be angry at my parents. They were my parents and I *had* to "honor" them, no matter what they did to me. God said so.

A Cross to Bear

In the spring of my junior year, I made one more trek to Cape Cod. Since I knew no one who could mediate, I decided I would talk with my parents directly, to see if there could be some way to change the relationship. This time, I didn't have to ride on buses to get there. By then, I had met Jim and we planned to marry. Jim had a car and so he drove. Once again I was very afraid, but this time, I wasn't going alone.

When I did speak to my parents, I did my best to speak my truth without accusations and to say: "This is what I felt like when I was growing up in this house."

The words I remember best from that painful visit were my mother's words when she said: "If there has ever been any problem in this family, it's your fault."

On our long drive back from the Cape to Amherst, I made a decision. I would not accept that identity in the family. I knew it wasn't true and had never been true.

The next time I met with Mr. Brown, I told him what had happened. I also told him that I had decided that I would not try again. Except for the fact that I was still legally a minor in a state where the age of majority was twenty-one, I was on my own.

I will never forget the disapproval in his eyes when he looked at me and told me: "Your first responsibility is to your parents. No matter how they treat you, you must forgive them and repent of your anger at them."

I remember using this metaphor to say to him: "It feels like trying to swim with a hundred pound weight on my back. I don't think I am strong enough to become what I want to be if I am under constant attack."

Mr. Brown said: "That is your cross to bear."

I said to him: "If that is what it means to be a Christian, I am no longer a Christian. I will not allow myself to be abused any more."

After that conversation, I stayed away from church for the next ten years. How and why I went back to church, and then on to theological seminary and graduate school in biblical studies, and then on to teach in theological seminaries, and even to hold clergy credentials for a while, is a long story, which will remain untold here.

When Authority Matters More Than Wellbeing

With the benefit of hindsight and perspective gained from my years of study in seminary, graduate school, teaching experience in seminaries, and my work in various churches, I came to understand that the overwhelming tendency of the Christian church is to reduce the most vulnerable people to roles and to insist that they must obey authority, with little regard for their own wellbeing.

I tell my own story here because it demonstrates this tendency. The particularities of my life didn't matter to Mr. Brown, even as my own life experiences didn't matter to Mr. Edwards. Even at the age of twenty, I heard that my "first responsibility" was to be obedient to a role in a relationship that had always been destructive to me. All that mattered was that I "obey" my parents, even though by every reasonable standard they were terrible parents. I was the one who had to repent for the sin of disobedience because I was not willing to submit to my role as the obedient daughter and allow myself to be abused without complaint. There is nothing redemptive in all of this for anyone.

Over the years since, struggling Christians and former Christians told me stories of their own experiences. Among others, battered women told me about going to their pastors and ministers for help, only to hear that that the solution was to be more submissive, because "the Bible says that wives must be submissive to their husbands." Gay people told me how they had been cut off from families and churches, because of their "abominable sinfulness." Black Christians told me of the racism they encountered in churches, based on "what the Bible says." All of this demonstrates use of the Bible used as a weapon against the innocent.

For many of these of these people, the solution was to leave the Christian church, not because they "wandered off," or "stumbled," or "tripped and fell into sin," but because their churches could offer them nothing except forgiveness of sin for their wounds, all done in the name of God, by misusing words from the Bible.

- I submit my story to you as an example of what it means for religion to trap little ones, to block the way, or to lead astray the innocent.

- This is the story of the deaf boys raped by a priest and offered forgiveness for their sins.

- This is the story of the child Augustine, who was beaten by his teachers, and received no help.

- This is the story of battered women who ask for help and get only commands to obey the ones who batter them.

- This is the story of gay Christians who are denounced and excluded for their sexuality.

- This is the story of human beings who are abused, excluded, demeaned, enslaved, and killed because of skin color.

The parabolic vision of the kingdom of heaven that Jesus offers in the Gospel of Matthew does not tolerate such abuse in the name of obedience. It's a vision of justice for the little ones. It's also a vision in which "belief and faith" do not require surrender to such treatment in the name of obedience to roles.

Part Eight

Freedom

To Become

Your True Self

Chapter 26
Symptoms of Your False Identity

> What you know you can't explain, but
> you feel it. You've felt it your entire life,
> that there's something wrong with the
> world. You don't know what it is, but it's
> there, like a splinter in your mind,
> driving you mad.
>
> Morpheus, *The Matrix* film

The Mirror of Sin and Subliminal Persuasion

The Christian doctrine of salvation from sin is so deeply
embedded in Western culture that it has become a defining
mirror for the world. You look at yourself in that mirror
and you think that you are seeing an accurate reflection of
your true identity.

The subliminal persuasion of this image is so powerful
that you believe it without question. What you see in the
mirror is the way things are, the way you are. You are a
defective being, who must be forgiven for being defective.
You must submit to authority, fulfilling your roles—roles
that are determined by your age, your sex, your family
relationships, and your social status.

Unconscious Assumptions of an Epoch

The effectiveness of this subliminal persuasion has become
so much a part of the collective Western worldview that it
has become unquestioned belief. Even if you consciously
reject Christian theology, this collective belief is so

powerful that it lurks in the shadows in a culture so thoroughly conditioned by salvation doctrine. You can change your thoughts but somehow, the belief lingers, the belief that there really is something wrong with you.

Beliefs are much tougher to eradicate than thoughts. By definition, you can't prove a belief. You believe something is true because you believe it is true. But beliefs always rest on assumptions, which are often unexamined. Alfred North Whitehead, mathematician and philosopher, claimed that every epoch has its unconscious assumptions:

> When you are criticizing the philosophy of an epoch, do not chiefly direct your attention to those intellectual positions which its exponents feel it necessary explicitly to defend. There will be some fundamental assumptions which adherents of all the variant systems within the epoch unconsciously presuppose.
>
> Such assumptions appear so obvious that people do not know what they are assuming because no other way of putting things has ever occurred to them.
>
> With these assumptions a certain limited number of types of philosophic systems are possible, and this group of systems constitutes the philosophy of the epoch (Whitehead 2010).

Christian salvation doctrine is one such assumption that appears "so obvious" in our epoch. Even if seekers look outside the Christian church, they take the church with them, even if they have the sense that there is something "wrong" with church.

If this is your experience, the nagging belief becomes a splinter in your mind, the lingering sense, that maybe they are right. You are defective and God is the Santa Claus in the sky who is making a list about whether you are naughty or nice.

What You See Is What You Get

The fundamental unquestioned assumptions lying beneath such unquestioned beliefs are problems of vision.

At the beginning of my first year in college, I attended a mixer put on by the university. It was an opportunity for students to meet each other as we wandered around a large ballroom filled with other new students.

I remember only one conversion from that mixer. In his effort to start a conversation, a student wearing glasses with thick lenses told me that he first started wearing glasses in first grade. A vision test at school revealed that he had very impaired vision. I remember that conversion because of this comment: "I didn't know there was something wrong my vision until I got my glasses. I thought everyone saw the world the way I did."

Everything you see is a vision *through your own eyes*. There is no such thing as a neutral observer. When you realize that the only way you see anything is through your own eyes, you also realize that there is no way of knowing whether what you see is accurate or whether it is a distortion. You cannot see anything "as it is." That is the fundamental insight of post-modernism.

So how can you know if you are seeing the world with impaired vision? How can you know that something is wrong with the world as you see it?

A Simple Test

Unlike the student who looked at the world for six years before he discovered that there was something wrong with his vision, there is actually a simple diagnostic test that can help you discern the difference.

It takes the form of four questions you ask when you feel stuck, confused, or torn between options.

A vivid example of the power of these questions is an experience with one of my students in a class on the Old

Testament Prophets at a theological seminary in Berkeley, California. Theological seminaries are graduate schools and so all of my students had at least one college degree. Several had more than one. One of my students was a young man I'll call Chris. Chris was a teacher's dream. Intelligent, thoughtful, considerate, personable, hardworking, he was a real asset in class discussions.

I gave my students short writing assignments for each class, to keep them involved in the material. My students were to write from one paragraph to one page on a specific assignment. I asked them to engage with the material, and do their best to answer the questions in the assignment without relying on secondary sources. I told them that I would not put grades on the assignments, but I would write comments. My class motto was: *It's never about getting the right answer.*

I noticed that Chris was not turning in his assignments and wondered why he, of all my students, was not doing his homework.

Chris showed up at my office hours one day to talk about the missing assignments. He said: "I don't understand what's wrong. I love your class. I love the material. I love the way you teach. But every time I sit down to write the assignment, I just can't do it. I don't know why. I don't have any trouble doing my homework for any of my other classes."

Four Questions

I asked if he wanted to figure out what was stopping him by answering four questions. He agreed.

Why should you?

I asked the first question: "Chris, why "should" you do these assignments?" He answered that question easily. He rattled off several reasons why he "should" do the assignments for the course. He talked about course requirements, and how his future plans depended on getting good grades, and how not doing the assignments would affect his grade point average.

Why do you refuse?

I then asked the second question: "Chris, instead of saying that you *can't* do the assignments, let's assume that there is a part of you—your true self—who *refuses* to do the assignments. It's not that you can't do them. Your true self refuses to do them because doing the assignments feels like a violation of itself.

Chris looked at me wide-eyed. He insisted that he was not refusing to do the assignments. He wanted to do them, but he just couldn't. But I asked him again: "Chris, why are you refusing to do these assignments?"

Chris continued to protest that he wasn't refusing, and then he suddenly stopped and leaned forward. At that moment, I knew we were about to strike pay dirt. In a deeper tone of voice, he made what sounded like a confession. He said: "I'm a poet. I write poetry. Every time I read the Hebrew prophets, I feel like writing a poem. But I know I shouldn't include a poem in an academic paper, and then I can't write anything."

There it was. His true self was a poet and wanted to write a poem. But when Chris decided that he "shouldn't" include poetry in an academic assignment, his true self said in effect: "No poetry, no assignment."

As soon as the problem was revealed, the solution was easy. I told Chris that the Hebrew prophets were poets and much of the material he was reading was poetry. I stated my opinion that the most authentic response to a poem is another poem. So, when Chris, the poet, wanted to write a poem in response to the poetry he was reading, I thought that was the most appropriate and authentic response possible.

Then I asked this question: "Chris, what makes you think you "shouldn't" include poetry in an academic assignment? All I care about with these assignments is that you engage with the material. I'm not looking for "right" answers. I don't want secondhand comments. All I ask is for you to tell me what you see when you ask particular questions. If you want to write a poem, write a poem."

Chris responded with an astonished, "Really?"

I said, "Really."

Why would you love to?

And then I said, "Chris, it's time for the third question. Why would you *love* to do these assignments?"

Chris answered easily. He found the material fascinating. He was intrigued by the stories. He was emotionally drawn into the words of the prophets. He spoke for several minutes about why he would love to do the assignments.

Why would you not love to?

I knew I didn't have to ask the fourth question: "Why would you NOT love to do the assignments?"

The Real Source of the Problem

At the next class session, Chris turned in all of the past assignments and was never late again for the rest of the semester. Each time I got a new stack of papers, I paged through them to find Chris's paper and put it on the bottom of the stack. After I read all of the other papers, I would pick up Chris's paper and say to myself, "I wonder what my poet has for me today." Chris's paper was dessert. Every time, he had some extraordinary insight about what he had read. A metaphor. A story. A poem. A photograph. Whatever it was, Chris was no longer stuck, unable to do his homework assignments.

You might not be a poet, but I am convinced that anytime you experience this kind of conflict between what you think you "should" do and your success at getting it done, the "I can't" is really, "I won't." For some reason, your true self is refusing to do the thing you "should" do because doing it would violate your true self.

I also believe that underneath the refusal, you will find a false assumption. For Chris, the false assumption was that he couldn't include his poetry in an academic assignment. How could a poet write authentically about poetry when he was not allowed to write as a poet? As soon as he understood that the assumption itself was false, he was no longer stuck. When his true self could write authentically, he had no trouble writing.

It's often that simple. The second question is the one that requires digging. I have seen it again and again, both in myself and in my students. If you're stuck, your true self is refusing to do what you think you "should" do, and the "should" is usually based on some false assumption. As soon as you uncover the false assumption, stuckness disappears.

I first found a version of these questions in *On Writer's Block*, by Victoria Nelson (Nelson 42). Nelson identifies the one who refuses as the "inner child." I find it much more effective and empowering to seek out the perspective of the "true self" rather than the "inner child."

Nelson also stops at three questions. I add a fourth question. "Why would you NOT love to do this?" This gives your true self the choice to do or not do what you are telling yourself you "should" do.

Stuckness as a Clue

The kind of stuckness that Chris experienced is a clue that your true self is clamoring to be heard. It refuses to obey the "should" because the "should" violates itself in some way. The key word in all of this is *refuse*.

Words matter. The words you use define your world, and they define your place in the world. Sometimes the solution to your stuckness is as simple as changing one word, just as changing one word in a Bible translation can either obscure or reveal meanings that run counter to the sin theology that has so shaped Western consciousness.

Against Your Own Best Interests

One of my ongoing life questions is: How is that we are so easily persuaded to act against our own best interests?

- How are we so easily persuaded to be obedient to those who claim authority over us?

- Why do we so easily surrender our hopes, our dreams, and our wants in the name of obedience?

- Why do we so readily look outside ourselves for what we "should" do rather than pay attention to what we would "love" to do?

- Why are we so willing to surrender to those who promise to save us rather than to become our own heroes and save ourselves?

The answers to these questions lie in the process of subliminal persuasion. The dominant assumption of the Christian epoch, based on the overwhelming influence of the doctrine of original sin in Western culture, is that to be human is to be flawed. You cannot save yourself. You must be saved *from* yourself.

Sin theology claims that our true selves are the ones we see in the mirror of original sin. It claims that our true selves are defective, selfish, disobedient, and proud. In a system shaped by the idea that believers must "come to worship" and "leave to minister," even asking why your true self refuses to do what it "should" do is a sign of sin.

At this point, no one has to persuade you, because you already believe it. If you have lived in Western culture, you have lived your entire life immersed in sin theology. Just as fish live their lives immersed in an ocean of water, we humans live our lives immersed in an "ocean" of air. This doctrine holds subliminal power over you even if you consciously reject the whole idea.

The first step to freedom from the pervasive effect of sin theology is to recognize how much this Christian salvation theology is a defective construction imposed on the Bible. It is not an accurate assessment of who you are.

Chapter 27
Claim Your Perfect Identity

No one can make you feel inferior
without your consent.

Eleanor Roosevelt

The Moment of Choice

The purpose of *Your True Self Identity* is to show you that
much of what the Christian church claims to be true about
your identity is based on theological constructions that
have less to do with the Bible than they have to do with the
religions, and the politics of religion, as they evolved over
the centuries in the Greco-Roman world.

But beyond this purpose, there is something deeper at
work here. James Ryan, in *Screenwriting from the Heart*,
claims that every screenplay is about one central dramatic
question. Everything in the story leads up to a moment of
decision. The same principle applies to stories. Every hero's
journey is a series of actions and choices leading up to one
final moment of choice.

If you have come this far, it's time for you to make a
decision based on the central question of this journey: Will
you choose to remain trapped in a false identity created by
centuries of Christian sin theology or will you choose to
claim your true identity?

It really is a matter of choice. You can choose to allow
yourself to be defined by theological doctrines and
traditions that tell you that you are flawed in your essence
because you are human, or you can recognize how these

theological doctrines and traditions trap you in a false identity.

The saying attributed to Eleanor Roosevelt, "No one can make you feel inferior without your consent," captures the essence of the decision. When you are aware that you really do have such a choice, you can consent to the false identity imposed upon you by the salvation claims of the Christian church or you can refuse to consent and claim your true identity. Your true identity called also be called your *perfect* identity.

But what is your perfect identity?

If You Wish to Be Perfect

Twice in the Gospel of Matthew, Jesus uses a particular word when he speaks about what it means to be a disciple.

The first occurrence is part of the collection of teachings called the Sermon on the Mount. The KJV and the NRSV translate as *perfect*. The CEB translates as *complete*:

> Be ye therefore perfect [*téleios*], even as your Father which is in heaven is perfect (Matthew 5:48, KJV).

> Be perfect, therefore, as your heavenly Father is perfect [*téleios*] (Matthew 5:48, NRSV).

> Therefore, just as your heavenly Father is complete [*téleios*] in showing love to everyone, so also must you be complete [*téleioi*] (Matthew 5:48, CEB).

The second occurs in the story about the rich young man, which is so often misinterpreted to assert: "Jesus said a rich man can't get into heaven." Once again, the KJV and NRSV translate as *perfect* and the CEB translates as *complete*:

> Jesus said unto him, If thou wilt be perfect [*téleios*], go [and] sell that thou hast, and give to the poor, and

thou shalt have treasure in heaven: and come [and] follow me (Matthew 19:21, KJV).

Jesus said to him, "If you wish to be perfect [*téleios*], go, sell your possessions, and give the money to the poor, and you will have treasure in heaven; then come, follow me" (Matthew 19:21, NRSV).

Jesus said, "If you want to be complete [*téleios*], go, sell what you own, and give the money to the poor. Then you will have treasure in heaven. And come follow me" (Matthew 19:21, CEB).

What Is Perfect?

What does it mean for you to be *perfect?*

Consider how *Dictionary.com* defines perfect in contemporary English:

- conforming absolutely to the description or definition of an ideal type

- excellent or complete beyond practical or theoretical improvement

- exactly fitting the need in a certain situation or for a certain purpose

- entirely without any flaws, defects, or shortcomings

- accurate, exact, or correct in every detail

If you read these definitions carefully, you will see that four of them are about meeting some sort of flawless ideal. If this is what *perfect* means, no human being can ever be that kind of perfect, unless you consider models in fashion magazines, with their skin, hair, and bodies airbrushed to a state of flawlessness never seen in real human beings.

The idea that you must meet some ideal standard of perfection—particularly the idea that you must be perfect as God is perfect—is a prescription for an endless sense of failure.

What Is Complete?

How about the word *complete*? What does it mean for you to be complete? Here's how *Dictionary.com* defines complete in contemporary English:

- having all parts or elements; lacking nothing; whole; entire; full.

- finished; ended; concluded.

- having all the required or customary characteristics, skills, or the like; consummate; perfect in kind or quality

- thorough; entire; total; undivided, uncompromised, or unmodified

If you read these definitions of complete carefully, you will a range of meanings, from being *whole*, to being *finished*, to being *perfect* in the sense of being flawless.

What Does This Mean in Greek?

In both Matthew 5:48 and 19:21, the words are adjectives based on the noun *télos*. The Greek words are the plural *téleioi* (5:48) and the singular *téleios* (19:21).

Télos means *end* In English, end can refer to both the termination of something and the purpose of something. Greek also has both connotations. *Télos* can be the *goal*, *purpose*, or *objective*. *Télos* can be the *result*, *outcome*, or *finish*:

- As an adjective, the ones who are *téleioi* are the ones who have accomplished the goal, achieved the purpose, finished the job.

- They are the ones who are whole, complete, fully developed.

- Greek also used the word to describe those who are adult, mature, fully-grown.

- And, the word can also have the connotation of meeting an ideal standard.

Teleology

In addition, *télos* defines a significant topic in philosophy and theology. *Teleology* refers to the *end* or *purpose* of nature. The fundamental teleological idea is that nature operates according to a purpose.

Teleological arguments to prove the existence of God go back to Greek philosophy and numerous early Christian writers, including Augustine, and continued in Western philosophy and theology.

A teleological argument is the foundation of the claim of creationists against evolution. They argue that the universe was created by "intelligent design" for a purpose, rather than by random occurrences in nature.

Teleology is also at the heart of the Christian gospels, and is evident throughout Matthew's Gospel. The meaning of *téleioi* in Matthew 5:48 and *téleios* 19:21 refers to a completed, undivided state of being, rather than a state of error-free perfection.

Flawless or Complete?

If you look at the five dictionary definitions of perfect in English above, all but the third definition conjure up notions of being ideal, flawless, and without error. The third definition, "exactly fitting the need in a certain situation or for a certain purpose," comes closest to the connotation of *téleioi* in Matthew because it refers to fulfilling your purpose.

In this case, the CEB translation as "complete" comes closer to capturing the meaning of *téleioi* and *téleios* in Matthew.

However, once again, the CEB has gone beyond translation in Matthew 5:48 by adding words that are not present in the Greek. The phrase "in showing love to everyone" is yet another gloss that is a commentary rather than a translation.

CEB has also added the word "must," which turns the verse into obligation.

Do You Have To?

The verb in 5:48 is *'ésesthe, to be*. Here it is an indicative, future verb in the second person plural. Although most translations turn the verb into an imperative, this it is not an imperative form. The verb has the sense of becoming something in the future, without the implied threat of "must."

Although I don't claim to know the original connotation of this verbal form in the Gospel of Matthew, I suggest the strong possibility that this is simply a straightforward future indicative of what you *can* become, without the implied obligation that you "have to" become something.

To Be Whole

I also suggest that using the word *whole* rather than *complete* provides a liberating insight into the meaning of *téleioi* and *téleios*. The word whole conveys the sense that you are undivided within yourself, even if you are not yet all that you can or will become. The word whole also frees you from the sense that you have to be "flawless."

With these substitutions, marked with italics, the NRSV translations become:

- You will become *whole,* just as your heavenly Father is *whole* (Matthew 5:48, NRSV revised by KRS).

- Jesus said to him, "If you wish to *become whole,* go, sell your possessions, and give the money to the poor, and you will have treasure in heaven; then come, follow me" (Matthew 19:21, NRSV revised by KRS).

Perfectly Whole

As an example of the difference I intend between whole and complete, I recently walked from the far end of a large parking lot into a supermarket behind a family of three— Mom, Dad, and a little boy, who was about four. The little boy caught my attention, and I observed him for a few moments. He was clearly at home in his small body, having mastered the fine arts of walking and jumping and talking. He seemed happy, engaged, and fully present. My impression from that brief observation was: This is a well-loved child, who is at home in his body, at home in his world, full of energy and awareness, and full of life and love. In other words, he was wholly perfect and perfectly whole.

But at the age of four, he has a lot more life to live and a lot more to learn. He is not yet *complete* in the sense of being everything that he can be, or will be, in what I truly hope is a long, happy, healthy, and productive life.

The word *holy* means *whole.* Holiness is not about following rules, but about being undivided. This is why Hebrew concepts of holiness are defined by concerns with purity and cleanness. All of the dietary laws and rituals are fundamentally about not mixing categories. In this theological system, God is holy because God is undivided.

This is the sense of what I mean by whole. You are whole when you are not at war with yourself, when you are not in a constant inner conflict between what you think you "should" do and what you desire to do. You can be whole even if your life is full of incomplete dreams and goals. You can be whole even if you experience failures and setbacks.

A House Divided

One of the best-known metaphors of Jesus is the image of a house divided against itself. Abraham Lincoln used this language in a speech in 1858 about the impossibility of maintaining a Union comprising both free states and slave states.

Jesus used the imagery of a house divided against itself in a confrontation with the Pharisees who claimed that Jesus was casting out demons by Beelzebul, the ruler of demons. Jesus refutes their argument with this statement:

> He knew what they were thinking and said to them,
> "Every kingdom divided against itself is laid waste,
> and no city or house divided against itself will stand"
> (Matthew 12:25, NRSV).

Jesus could have expanded the metaphor to include persons divided against themselves. If you are divided within yourself, you will have a difficult time standing your ground.

A Clue

One of the best ways to know whether or not you are divided against yourself is to pay attention to your words. I admit that I have a strong bias against one of the most common words in the English language. It is the word "should," and its cousins, "ought," "must," "have to." Sometimes, they come with a "not" attached. Then they yammer at you about what you "should not" do, "ought not" do, "must not" do.

I do my best to avoid using the language of "should," in what I say to other people and what I say to myself. When I do use it in writing, I mark it with quotation marks, to set it off from other words. And if I ever hear myself say one of these words out loud or in my own head, I consciously cancel it out immediately.

Why do I have such a bias against this word? It's because "should" and "should not" and their bossy pals are invaders, sent by someone else to impose someone else's will upon your life.

That's bad enough, but soon the invaders take up residence, and you start using those words upon yourself. If you listen to yourself when you feel stuck, or if you listen to other people who are complaining about being stuck, simply pay attention to how often you hear these words. The truth is that you create your world with your words. A world constructed with these words is a world of conflict, confusion, and doubt.

Your Conditioned Self

The experience of feeling stuck is often evidence of a "should" based on a false assumption. This was the situation of my student Chris, who "couldn't do" his homework assignments because he "shouldn't" include poetry in an academic assignment.

Where does "should" come from, and why is it so powerful? "Should" is the language of the conditioned self. The conditioned self learned to survive in this world by being obedient to external authority. We all started out that way. As small children, we had no other frame of reference beyond the towering adults in our small worlds, adults who used "should" and "should not" copiously.

The first goal of the conditioned self is to protect itself from harm or destruction, motivated by the innate desire to stay alive. Your conditioned self is relentless in its desire to protect you from harm. This is why people so often run into obstacles when they decide to do something that means stepping out of bounds. It can be dangerous for you when you challenge the "shoulds" and "should nots" of your world, when the enforcers are more powerful than you are.

This is why stuckness is often evidence of a conflict between the conditioned self and the true self over obedience. Do you obey outer authority or your true self? Do you do what you really want to do or do you do what "they" want you to do?

The Ties That Bind

This is especially true when it comes to religion. When it comes to anything related to the Bible and religion, "should" and "authority" are tightly bound together.

The word *religion* is derived from the Latin *re* (back) and *ligare* (bind). Religion is about obligation. By the way, *obligation* is derived from *ob* (to) and *ligare* (bind). The same root occurs in *ligament* and *ligature* and *rely*. They are all about tying something to something else. Religion *binds you back* and obligation *binds you to* the authority of your own tradition.

While we're at it, let's take a look at the word *authority*. Both *author* and *authority* come from the same Latin root, *auctor*, which refers to the power to give commands and enforce obedience. The one with authority is the one who can tell you what you *must* do and enforce your compliance.

All of this binding takes place in the language of "should" and its bossy, know-it-all cousins. This is why the language of "should" and "should not" and "must" and "must not" is so deeply "tied up" and "tied back" and "tied to" religious traditions, including reading of the Bible.

However, when it comes to religion and the Bible, it's not just the big people in your world who tell you what you "should" do. They have God on their side, and God holds the ultimate trump card. Obey authority or you will be punished, not just in this life, but for eternity.

Freedom from the Identity Concealment Program

Let's go back to where we started, with Dave Lakhani's reference to false identities. In a witness protection program, the false identity protects you from harm because you know too much.

In contrast, the dominant tendency of the Christian church, in its vast array of permutations, is to enroll you in an identity concealment program under a false identity that hides your true identity from you.

By and large, the Christian church has done a terrible job of teaching people to be true to our own selves. The most damaging misuse of the Gospel stories is that they rob believers of the greatest realization contained within every hero's journey story. By identifying believers as flawed beings who need to be saved, the church deprives believers of the central truth of every hero's journey story. The hero already has the capacity to do the task.

This is the benefit of reading hero's journey stories. They give us visions of our own possibilities. I like the way these two authors put it:

> Without heroes, we are all plain people, and don't know how far we can go (Bernard Malamud).
>
> Heroes take journeys, confront dragons, and discover the treasure of their true selves (Carol Lynn Pearson).

As long as Jesus is the only perfect human—the only one who can save you from your flawed self—you are cheated out of the realization that you are more than you imagine yourself.

I remember one woman in a church I used to attend who kept saying things like, "I am nothing. It's all God," as she proclaimed again and again that she was not capable of anything. It was a strange combination of boasting in the name of humility. In her vision of herself, she was nothing more than God's puppet on strings.

Freedom Is an Inside Job

What is the solution? The key to the freedom to be your true self is the realization at the heart of every hero's journey. Freedom is not something that anyone can give you from the outside. Freedom is an inside job. It comes when you claim it. You claim it when you refuse to accept the false identity foisted upon you by theological doctrines and church practices that are soaked in sin juice.

In the midpoint of the hero's journey called the Gospel of Matthew, Jesus undergoes a transformative experience. This experience is the transfiguration, the moment of metamorphosis. The relevant question is, what was transformed? Was it Jesus himself or was it his perception of himself?

Up to that point in the story, Matthew has identified Jesus with the subtlety of a tank knocking down a brick wall. Jesus is the Messiah. Jesus is the Beloved Son of God. The turning point in Jesus' hero's journey is the moment when Jesus truly accepts his identity. Only then is he willing to head to Jerusalem to fulfill his hero's mission.

The *Wizard of Oz* is also hero's journey story. Dorothy heads off along the Yellow Brick Road on her hero's journey to see the Wizard, believing that only the Wizard can send her home again. Dorothy becomes her own hero when she realizes that she always had what she needed to find her way back home. Her companions on the journey, the Tin Man, the Cowardly Lion, and the Scarecrow, come to the same realization. They are looking outside themselves for what they already have within them.

By making Jesus the only hero, the only savior, the only perfect human, the Christian church robs believers of the liberating gift at the heart of every hero's journey. This is the insight in one of my favorite movies, the silliest profound story I know:

> I am my only hope for a hero (Joe, *Joe Versus the Volcano*).

Your Choice

We have come back to the central question of this journey. Will you choose to remain trapped in a false identity created by centuries of Christian theology or will you choose to claim your true identity?

If all you see when you look in the mirror is a flawed being who must be saved from your sinful nature, you will live the life of Augustine. You might become a saint, but it will be a "sainted" life full of self-hatred, doubt, and fear in an identity created by shame.

Make it as theological as you want, but if you have to be "saved" from your human self, you will remain in a salvation trap that prevents you from living as a whole person in this life.

It really is a matter of choice. You can choose to allow yourself to be defined by theological doctrines and traditions that tell you that you are flawed in your essence because you are human, or you can recognize how these theological doctrines and traditions trap you in a false identity.

Freedom to Be Your True Self

Freedom to be your true self is as simple and as difficult as refusing to obey the kind of authority that violates your true self.

It's simple when you realize how much of what you "should" do is a flimflam construction of theologies imposed on the Bible. This brief look at the Gospel of Matthew has demonstrated just a few ways in which Christian tradition has turned the Gospel stories upside down, to turn stories intended to liberate the little ones into weapons of shame against them.

At the same time, setting yourself free from the salvation trap can be extremely difficult. Your conditioned self learned all too well that survival meant obedience to those who had power over you. They taught you so well that their "shoulds" are now your "shoulds." You don't need anyone else to tell you what you "should" do if you are constantly telling yourself what you "should" do.

The best way to cut yourself loose from the warnings of your conditioned self is to understand how the conditioned self is so often a false guide. It might have your best interests at heart, but it doesn't have all the facts.

Here is the moment of decision. Will you continue to allow the mishmash of doctrines, translations, church dogmas, church structures, and church practices to define you with an identity of shame, which keeps you divided and stuck? Or will you use of the model of the hero's journey in the Gospel of Matthew to become your own hero, claim your perfect identity as a whole person, and become your true self?

Postlogue
Seeing Your True Self Identity

Sometimes you've got to let everything
go - purge yourself. If you are unhappy
with anything . . . whatever is bringing
you down, get rid of it. Because you'll
find that when you're free, your true
creativity, your true self comes out.

Tina Turner

Reflections in a Mirror

Years ago I read an article by an anthropologist who discovered a small tribe living in some remote area. He told how he took a photograph of the whole group and showed it to the people. Everyone who looked at the picture recognized every person in the picture except one. The one unrecognized person was always the person who was looking at the photo.

In our world filled with mirrors and cameras, can you imagine living your life in a world where you have never seen your own image?

The truth is that you cannot see yourself as you are. You can only see what is reflected back to you in mirror images or captured in photographs or as digital images on screens or through the eyes of others.

The story of the ugly duckling is also a story about reflections in a mirror—in this case the mirror of the clear water of a stream. The story of the ugly duckling ends when the spring comes and the frozen water melts. When the ice melts, the water becomes a mirror for the "ugly duckling":

It would be very sad, were I to relate all the misery and privations which the poor little duckling endured during the hard winter; but when it had passed, he found himself lying one morning in a moor, amongst the rushes. He felt the warm sun shining, and heard the lark singing, and saw that all around was beautiful spring. Then the young bird felt that his wings were strong, as he flapped them against his sides, and rose high into the air. They bore him onwards, until he found himself in a large garden, before he well knew how it had happened. The apple-trees were in full blossom, and the fragrant elders bent their long green branches down to the stream which wound round a smooth lawn. Everything looked beautiful, in the freshness of early spring. From a thicket close by came three beautiful white swans, rustling their feathers, and swimming lightly over the smooth water. The duckling remembered the lovely birds, and felt more strangely unhappy than ever.

"I will fly to those royal birds," he exclaimed, "and they will kill me, because I am so ugly, and dare to approach them; but it does not matter: better be killed by them than pecked by the ducks, beaten by the hens, pushed about by the maiden who feeds the poultry, or starved with hunger in the winter."

Then he flew to the water, and swam towards the beautiful swans. The moment they espied the stranger, they rushed to meet him with outstretched wings.

"Kill me," said the poor bird; and he bent his head down to the surface of the water, and awaited death (Andersen, "The Ugly Duckling").

The Ugly Duckling's Transfiguration

What happens next is the moment of the ugly duckling's transfiguration. He actually sees himself for the first time as he truly is. For the first time in his miserable life, he knows his true identity. He is not an ugly duck. He is a beautiful swan:

> But what did he see in the clear stream below? His own image; no longer a dark, gray bird, ugly and disagreeable to look at, but a graceful and beautiful swan. To be born in a duck's nest, in a farmyard, is of no consequence to a bird, if it is hatched from a swan's egg. He now felt glad at having suffered sorrow and trouble, because it enabled him to enjoy so much better all the pleasure and happiness around him; for the great swans swam round the new-comer, and stroked his neck with their beaks, as a welcome.
>
> Into the garden presently came some little children, and threw bread and cake into the water.
>
> "See," cried the youngest, "there is a new one;" and the rest were delighted, and ran to their father and mother, dancing and clapping their hands, and shouting joyously, "There is another swan come; a new one has arrived."
>
> Then they threw more bread and cake into the water, and said, "The new one is the most beautiful of all; he is so young and pretty." And the old swans bowed their heads before him.
>
> Then he felt quite ashamed, and hid his head under his wing; for he did not know what to do, he was so happy, and yet not at all proud. He had been persecuted and despised for his ugliness, and now he heard them say he was the most beautiful of all the

birds. Even the elder-tree bent down its bows into the water before him, and the sun shone warm and bright. Then he rustled his feathers, curved his slender neck, and cried joyfully, from the depths of his heart, "I never dreamed of such happiness as this, while I was an ugly duckling" (Andersen, "The Ugly Duckling").

Reflections in a Theological Funhouse

The sin theology of the Christian church is so destructive because it holds up a mirror in front of you and says: "This is what you are. You are an ugly duckling."

All mirrors lie one way or another. However, the mirror of original sin is a funhouse mirror—except that there is nothing fun about it. Funhouse mirrors distort mirror images into grotesque reflections. Although it can be fun to go through a carnival funhouse and stare at your distorted image when you know what is happening, it's an entirely different experience when you believe that the grotesque shape in front of you is a true reflection of you.

This is what the mirror of original sin does. It distorts your image while insisting that it is an accurate reflection of your true nature. All you see in this mirror is a grotesque image of yourself without ever knowing that you are wandering through the maze of a theological funhouse.

The moment of transfiguration in the hero's journey of Jesus in the Gospel of Matthew is a moment when he sees himself in a mirror that is not a funhouse mirror. He sees himself and experiences himself as he truly is. Beloved and radiant, he sees his true self revealed for the first time.

When the Hero's Journey of Jesus Becomes Your Journey

If the transfiguration experience in the Gospel of Matthew is a historical event about the only perfect human who ever lived, the story doesn't have much to say to the rest of us, except to remind us that we are so imperfect that the only perfect man who ever lived had to die to "save" us from the sin of being ugly ducklings.

Whatever you believe to be true about Jesus, the journey of Jesus in the Gospel of Matthew can become a model of your own hero's journey to become your true self. Your own transformative moment can occur when you recognize yourself in the mirror as you are—already perfect and perfectly worthy of love, even if you are not yet all that you can become.

You don't have to change into something else. You need only see your true self reflected back to you through the eyes of love. Vision through eyes of love is a radically changed vision than the vision in the funhouse mirror of original sin.

The True Self Secret of Happiness

Although I am not persuaded that the ugly duckling would feel "...glad at having suffered sorrow and trouble, because it enabled him to enjoy so much better all the pleasure and happiness around him...," I do believe that there is a direct correlation between seeing an accurate reflection of your true self and being happy. You can never be happy if you believe that you are nothing but an ugly duckling.

The real secret of happiness that eludes so many of us lies in this simple story. Happiness is the result of a ridding process. You don't find happiness by changing into something you are not. Rather, you find happiness by getting rid of the conditioned beliefs of your false self. You become happy when you get rid of the distorting mirrors— especially the funhouse mirror of original sin—so that you can see yourself as you truly are. The moment when you see your true self is the moment of your own transfiguration. This is also the moment when you can experience the happiness of seeing your true self for the first time.

Go in Peace

I will end with one more story. I have told two stories about going to clergy to ask for help—the first a few days before my nineteenth birthday, and the second a year and a half later. In both cases, what I truly wanted was for someone to believe me as I told the truth of my life. The truth of my life is that I was the ugly duckling who experienced endless abuse, including the experience of being treated cruelly by my family because I was so "ugly." In my case, I really was called "ugly"—the exact words were, "the homeliest girl in the world"—again and again. Both the ugly duckling and I reached a point where we decided not to take it anymore. Each of us ran away.

With hindsight, I realize what I wanted most when I visited Mr. Edwards and Mr. Brown. I wanted each one to say in so many words: "Go in peace. It is not God's will for you to endure abuse." But I never heard such words from anyone in the Christian church until I met Sister Barbara.

Sister Barbara was a Roman Catholic sister, with a Ph.D. in political science from the University of California at Berkeley, who taught political science at a Catholic college. I saw Sister Barbara for almost a year for spiritual direction when I was in the last stages of my doctoral work. The major question of my life at that point concerned whether or not to stay within the Christian church, which was directly related to whether or not I would accept a tenure-track teaching position in a theological seminary.

Sister Barbara was the wisest, most peaceful, and most gently radiant Christian I have ever met. Hers wasn't the Bible-quoting smugness of Evangelical churches or the arm-waving, hallelujah-shouting enthusiasm of Pentecostal churches. I have experienced both types of those believers in various churches over the years. Instead, she embodied unconditional love and deep wisdom.

In one of our last meetings together, I told her that I had decided to leave the church. She said to me: "You are not leaving the church. You are taking care of yourself." It was the first time in my life when anyone within the Christian church even implied that taking care of myself was a higher priority than enduring abuse in obedience to rules.

After years of biblical study and teaching in theological seminaries, and after years of experience with numerous churches of various denominations, I have come to this one firm conviction: The only type of "God" worthy of being called *God* values your life more than your obedience. It is never "God's will" for you to be demeaned and abused because of who you are. Your life is precious because you are you. Even if you are not yet what you will become, you are not an "ugly duckling." That's true even if you really are a duck.

In many churches, the service ends with a benediction. A benediction is a blessing. The word itself means *to speak well of.* Words of blessing intend the best for another.

And so, wherever you are in your hero's journey to claim your true self identity, whether you are within the Christian church or have chosen to leave it, I leave you with these words:

> Go in peace. May you experience the happiness of the swan when he at last knows his true identity.

Kalinda Rose Stevenson. Ph.D.

References

Articles and Books

Andersen, Hans Christian. "The Ugly Duckling." *Fairy Tales and Stories*. Translated by H. P. Paull. http://hca.gilead.org.il/ugly_duc.html.

Bennett, Hal Zina. *Write From The Heart: Unleashing The Power Of Your Creativity*. Novato, CA: Nataraj Publishing, 1995.

Bonnet, James. *Stealing Fire From the Gods: The Complete Guide To Story For Writer's And Filmmakers*. 2nd ed. Studio City, CA: Michael Wiese Productions, 2006.

Boulding, Maria, trans. *The Confessions Of Saint Augustine*. New York: Vintage Books, 1998.

Brueggemann, Walter. "Biblical Authority." *Religion-Online.org*. http://www.religion-online.org/showarticle.asp?title=2104

Campbell, Joseph. *The Hero With A Thousand Faces*. Bollingen Series XVII. 2nd ed. Princeton, NJ: Princeton University Press, 1968.

Capps, Donald. *The Depleted Self: Sin In A Narcissistic Age*. Minneapolis: Fortress Press, 1998.

"Chinese Whispers." *Wikipedia*. http://en.wikipedia.org/wiki/Chinese_whispers.

Countryman, William. Biblical *Authority Or Biblical Tyranny? Scripture And The Christian Pilgrimage*. Philadelphia: Fortress Press, 1981.

"Fundamentalism." *Wikipedia*. http://en.wikipedia.org/wiki/Fundamentalism.

Harpur, Tom. *The Pagan Christ: Is Blind Faith Killing Christianity?* New York: Walker & Company, 2004.

Hoffman, Joel. "Five Mistakes in Your Bible Translation." *Huffington Post.* December 9, 2011. http://www.huffingtonpost.com/dr-joel-hoffman/five-mistakes-bible-translation_b_1129620.html.

Jefferson, Thomas. "Thomas Jefferson's Bible: The Life And Morals Of Jesus Of Nazareth.*" Smithsonian National Museum Of American History.* http://americanhistory.si.edu/jeffersonbible.

"Jesus Seminar." *Wikipedia.* http://en.wikipedia.org/wiki/Jesus_Seminar.

Lakhani, Dave. *Subliminal Persuasion: Influence And Marketing Secrets They Don't Want You To Know.* Hoboken, New Jersey: John Wiley & Sons, 2008.

Lenski, Gerhard E. *Power And Privilege: A Theory Of Social Stratification.* Chapel Hill: University Of North Carolina Press, 1984.

McFadyen, Alistair. *Bound To Sin: Abuse, Holocaust and the Christian Doctrine Of Original Sin.* Cambridge: Cambridge University Press, 2000.

Mitchell, Stephen. *The Gospel According To Jesus: A New Translation And Guide To His Essential Teachings For Believers And Unbelievers.* New York: HarperPerennial, 1993.

Nelson, Victoria. *On Writer's Block: A New Approach To Creativity.* New York: Houghton Mifflin Company, 1993.

Outler, Albert Cook, trans and ed. *The Confessions Of Saint Augustine.* Mineola, New York: Dover Publications, 2002.

Peck, M. Scott, M.D. *Further Along The Road Less Traveled: The Unending Journey Toward Spiritual Growth.* New York: Simon & Schuster, 1993.

Ryan, James. *Screenwriting From The Heart: The Techniques Of The Character-Driven Screenplay.* New York: Billboard Books, 2000.

Schrempp, Gregory. "What Is Myth?" *Folklore Connections.* Mary Magoulick. http://hercules.gcsu.edu/~mmagouli/defmyth.htm.

Vogler, Christopher. *The Writer's Journey: Mythic Structure For Writers.* 2nd ed. Studio City, CA: Michael Wiese Productions, 1998.

Waetjen, Herman. *A Reordering Of Power: A Socio-Political Reading of Mark's Gospel.* Minneapolis: Fortress Press, 1989.

Whitehead, Alfred North. "Margin Notes: Alfred North Whitehead from Heather Griffin." Marginal Conversations. October 7, 2010. http://www.marginalconversations.com/category/philosophy/alfred-north-whitehead

About the Author

Dr. Kalinda Rose Stevenson is an award-winning author, biblical scholar, and former teacher in theological seminaries. She offers a liberating perspective on the connection between mistranslated Bible verses and false identity. Her unique perspective provides solutions to overcome self-conflict, confusion, and shame caused by misuse of the mistranslated Bible verses.

She earned her Ph.D. in Biblical Studies at the Graduate Theological Union in Berkeley, California, in cooperation with the University of California at Berkeley.

She currently lives with her husband in the Las Vegas area of Nevada.

Find out more by visiting her websites
KalindaRoseStevenson.com
DoestheBibleReallySayThat.com

Index

H

T

www.ingramcontent.com/pod-product-compliance
Lightning Source LLC
Chambersburg PA
CBHW051940090426
42741CB00008B/1216